Guided Course in English Composition

T. C. Jupp and John Milne

Students' Book
New Edition

HEINEMANN

Heinemann International
a division of Heinemann Educational Books Ltd
Halley Court, Jordan Hill, Oxford OX2 8EJ

OXFORD   LONDON   EDINBURGH
MADRID   ATHENS   BOLOGNA
MELBOURNE   SYDNEY   AUCKLAND
IBADAN   GABORONE   NAIROBI
SINGAPORE   KINGSTON   PORTSMOUTH (NH)

ISBN 0 435 28497 5

© T. C. Jupp and John Milne 1969 and 1987
First published 1969 (reprinted ten times)
This edition 1988

A Teachers' Handbook is available with this course (ISBN 0 435 28498 3)

Acknowledgements
The authors and publishers would like to thank the following for permission to use photographic material:
Aerofilms Ltd (p. 18); Barnaby's Picture Library (pp. 13, 54, 55); London Borough of Bromley Central Library (p. 91); Milton Keynes Development Corporation (pp. 92, 93).

Illustrations by Neil Reed (pp. 6, 20, 34, 44, 50, 65, 77 and 83)
Maps and diagrams by John Gilkes (pp. 13, 29, 54, 59)
Handwriting by Richard Geiger
Cover by Stuart Hughes

Designed by Sue Vaudin
Phototypesetting by Goodfellow and Egan, Cambridge
Printed in Great Britain by
Butler & Tanner Ltd, Frome and London

90 91 92 93 94 10 9 8 7 6 5 4

Contents

UNIT 1

1 **Your education** p6
time clauses

2 **An interesting journey** p10
time clauses

3 **Your town or village** p15
because clauses
time clauses

4 **A wedding** p20
adjectival clauses
time clauses
because clauses

5 **Lost and found** p26
adjectival clauses
because clauses

6 **Planning and writing a free composition** p31

UNIT 2

7 **Wanting money for something** p34
so that clauses
adjectival clauses

8 **An important interview, examination or meeting** p39
noun clauses
so that clauses
adjectival clauses

9 **A theft** p44
noun clauses

10 **An imaginary holiday** p50
if clauses
noun clauses

11 **A letter giving travel instructions** p56
if clauses
noun clauses

12 **Planning and writing a free composition** p62

UNIT 3

13 **Young people starting work** p65
co-ordinate clauses
noun clauses
if clauses

14 **A strange story** p71
present participle phrases
if clauses
noun clauses
co-ordinate clauses

15 **Sports and games** p77
verb + (pro)noun + to + infinitive
although clauses
present participle phrases

16 **An important annual festival** p83
verbs in the passive
verb + (pro)noun + to + infinitive
although clauses

17 **Changes in your town or village** p89
infinitives of purpose
adjectival clauses

18 **Free compositions** p95

Introduction to new edition

Guided Course in English Composition develops accuracy and fluency in continuous writing through a series of eighteen graded compositions writing tasks, covering narrative, descriptive and discursive writing. By the end of the course, students will be able to produce substantial pieces of continuous writing on their own. The course is designed for intermediate students who are writing compositions for the first time or, if worked through more quickly, for more advanced students who want to develop their writing skills.

The course combines detailed guidance and preparation of language, subject matter and planning with the opportunity for personal expression and communication. The special emphasis of the course in terms of language is upon the use of a wide variety of clauses in complex sentences. The course also provides extensive wider practice; for example, in sentence structure, verg forms, adverbial and adjectival phrases. Students have to develop and use a wide range of vocabulary and to practise the conventions of written English, such as punctuation and lay-out. The emphasis of the course in terms of content is upon writing from personal experience. There is a balance and development between narrative writing, different sorts of descriptive writing and discursive writing. There is also some practice in letter writing. The emphasis of the course is on creating the opportunity for personal communication between students through group work and class sharing. By this means, an immediate and real 'audience' can be created for students' personal writing.

Each composition writing task is divided into four major stages:
— introduction, understanding and discussion of the subject
— intensive oral preparation of language and subject matter
— analysis of a sample composition in terms of language, content and sequence of content
— planning and writing of students' own work
— checking, sharing and correction of writing

The new edition preserves the general approach and philosophy of the original book, but has been changed and updated in five main ways:

1 More emphasis has been given to the introduction and planning of subject matter.

2 The analysis and planning of paragraph sequencing has been introduced from the beginning. There are also two compositions (six and twelve) which concentrate on understanding and planning different types of writing.

3 There has been some reduction of over rigid language control in the structure practices and sample compositions. However, the general approach to language remains one of clear control and guidance in respect of target structures for use in each writing task.

4 There has been extensive updating of content and layout.

A revised Teachers' Handbook is available for use with the Students' Book.

UNIT ONE
Composition 1

Subject: **Your education**

Write about the different schools and colleges you have attended. Mention the subjects you studied and the examinations you passed. Also, say something about the games you played and any other hobbies or other interests you had.

Introducing the subject

When did you first go to school?
How old were you?
How many different schools (and colleges) have you been to?
What subjects did you study at each?
What subjects did you like best?
What hobbies or interests did you have?

Structure practice

In this composition, you are going to practise sentences containing **time clauses** which begin with the words **when, before, after** and **while**.

Examples: **When I was five years old,** I started my education.
I studied for four hours every evening **while I was preparing for my final examinations**.

Use the sentences below to talk about your education. Work in pairs or groups. Try always to say things which really happened.

1 Complete
You can complete each sentence in many different ways.

> When I was ... years old, ...
> After I had studied for ... years in primary school, I ...
> While I was studying in primary school, ...
> Before I left school, I ...

Example: When I was eleven years old, I went to High School.

2 Ask and answer
You can answer each question in many different ways.

a | When were you given your first | school bag? / bicycle? / watch? / radio? / calculator? (etc.)

Example: I was given my first watch when I passed my final secondary school examination.

b | How did you feel | before you heard the result of / while you were studying for / after you heard the result of | your ... examination?

UNIT ONE: Composition 1

Example: | I felt very | excited / frightened / hopeful / worried | before I heard the result of my secondary school entrance examination.

c | What subjects did you study / What games did you play / Where did you live / What kind of clothes did you wear | when you were at | primary school? / intermediate school? / secondary school? / university? / teacher training college?

Example: I wore a school uniform when I was at secondary school.

3 Complete
You can complete each sentence in many different ways.

I began to learn English
I went to boarding school
I successfully passed all my examinations
I used to wear . . .
I had to travel . . . miles every day
I ate my lunch at home
I studied for . . . hours every evening

when . . .
before . . .
after . . .
while . . .

Example: I studied for four hours every evening while I was preparing for my final examination.

Sample composition

Read through the following:

My education
   I started primary school when I was five years old. My primary school was very close to my home. School started at quarter past nine in the morning and finished at half-past three in the afternoon. There was a lunchbreak from twelve o'clock to one o'clock and I used to go home for lunch. After I finished lunch, I used to run back to school as quickly as possible. Some other children did the same as me. We used to play football together in the playground before afternoon classes started again. When I was at primary school, I learned reading, writing and simple maths.
   When I was eleven, I sat the entrance examination to junior secondary school. I felt worried before I heard the result. I was very pleased when I heard that I had passed successfully. When I was at junior secondary school, I studied English, Maths, French, Latin, History and Geography. My favourite subject was English. The English teacher was very friendly and used to tell us interesting stories.

UNIT ONE: Composition 1

> When I was fourteen, I sat the entrance examination for senior secondary school. While I was waiting for the result, I again felt very worried. When I passed this examination, I was given my first bicycle. I had to cycle six miles to school every morning. After I went to senior secondary school, I studied very hard. For example, I did three hours homework every evening. While I was studying in the evenings, I often wanted to go out with my friends. My friends used to go out together on their bicycles. But I was not able to go with them. However, senior secondary school was not only hard work. At the weekends, I was able to have time off to play football and tennis.

Preparation and writing

1 **Structure practice**
   a Choose some sentences from the Structure Practice which you will be able to use in your composition.
   b Write them down in the order in which you will use them.

2 **Sample composition**
   a The Sample Composition has three paragraphs. What is each paragraph about?

Example: *Paragraph One – primary school.*

   b Write down two sentences containing a time clause from each paragraph.

3 **Your writing**
   a Read the subject on page 6.
   b Think about your education up till now. How many different schools or colleges have you attended? Decide how many paragraphs you are going to write.
   c Make notes on the contents of each paragraph. Decide when you will use the sentences you have written from the Structure Practice (1b above).
   d You may find it useful to refer to the Sample Composition while you are writing. Make sure you include several sentences containing time clauses in your composition.

4 **Checking your work**
   a Read through your writing carefully.
   b Exchange your work with another student.
   c Check each other's work for any mistakes.

UNIT ONE

Composition 2

Subject: **An interesting journey**

Write about a particularly interesting journey you once made. Explain why you made this journey and then describe the different stages of the journey. Mention what happened on the journey, and the places you saw or visited.

Introducing the subject
Has anyone been on an interesting journey recently?
What's the most interesting or exciting journey you have ever made?
Why did you make the journey?
How did you travel?
How long did the journey last?

Structure practice

In this composition, you are going to practise sentences containing **time clauses**. These clauses are introduced by **when, before, after, while** (as in Composition One) and by **until, as soon as** and **whenever**.

Examples: **As soon as the aeroplane started,** I felt very excited.
I waited in the cafe **until the bus came**.

Use the sentences and questions below to talk about your interesting journey. Work in pairs or groups. Try always to say things which really happened.

1 **Ask and answer**
You can answer each question in many different ways.

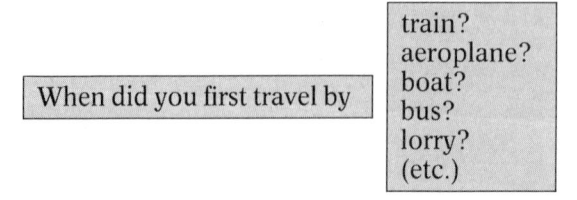

When did you first travel by | train? / aeroplane? / boat? / bus? / lorry? / (etc.)

Example: I first travelled by lorry when I hitch-hiked to London.

2 **Complete**
You can complete each sentence in many different ways.

a While I was | staying / living | in ..., I travelled from ... to ...

10

UNIT ONE: Composition 2

Example: While I was staying in Canada, I travelled from Vancouver to New York.

b After I had packed my luggage, ...

After I had bought my ticket, ...

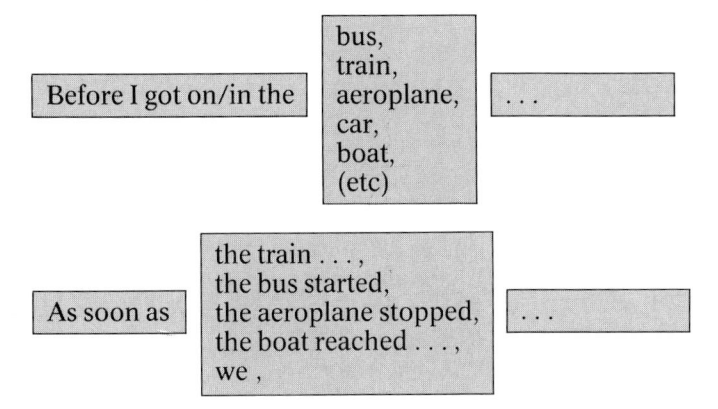

| Before I got on/in the | bus, train, aeroplane, car, boat, (etc) | ... |

| As soon as | the train ..., the bus started, the aeroplane stopped, the boat reached ..., we , | ... |

Whenever the ... stopped, ...

Example: After I had bought my ticket, I bought some sandwiches for the journey.

c | I felt very excited / I tried to go to sleep / I waited in / I read a book | while ... / when ... / whenever ... / until ... / before ... / after ... |

Example: I tried to go to sleep after it became dark.

3 Ask and answer
You can answer each question in many different ways.

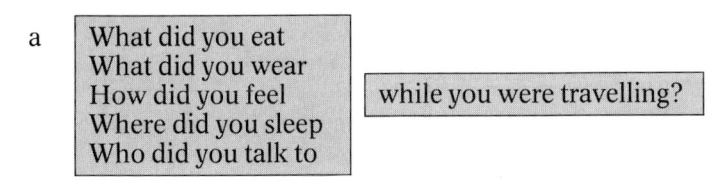

a | What did you eat / What did you wear / How did you feel / Where did you sleep / Who did you talk to | while you were travelling? |

Example: I felt very excited while I was travelling.

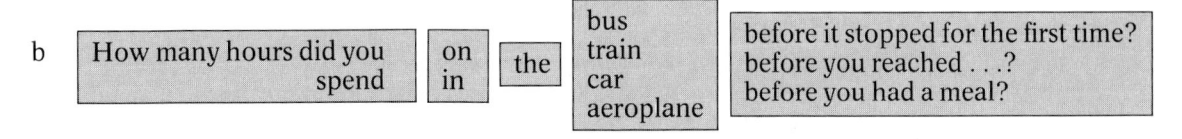

b | How many hours did you spend | on / in | the | bus / train / car / aeroplane | before it stopped for the first time? / before you reached ...? / before you had a meal? |

Example: I spent eight hours in the bus before it stopped for the first time.

11

UNIT ONE: Composition 2

4 **Complete**
You can complete each sentence in many different ways.

Think of some events which happened during the journey.

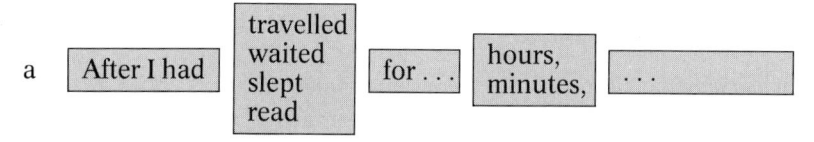

a After I had | travelled / waited / slept / read | for ... | hours, minutes, | ...

Example: After I had slept for three hours, the train suddenly stopped and we all had to get out.

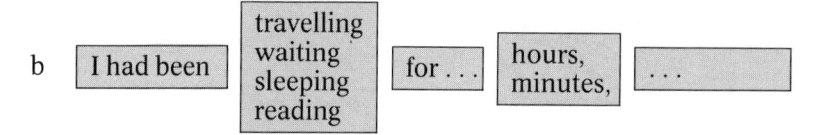

b I had been | travelling / waiting / sleeping / reading | for ... | hours, minutes, | ...

Example: I had been waiting for four hours, when the bus finally arrived.

Sample composition

Read through the following:

My journey from Vancouver to New York

When I was eighteen, I visited Canada for three months because my mother's family lived there. I stayed near Vancouver. Before I returned to England, I travelled all the way from Vancouver to New York by bus. This journey was the most interesting journey I have ever made.

The first stage of the journey was from Vancouver to Edmonton through the Rocky Mountains. We left Vancouver early in the morning. We spent eight hours on the bus before it stopped for the first time. While we were waiting at the stop, I bought a hamburger and a milk shake. After we left the stop, the scenery became very beautiful. I looked out of the window at lakes, mountains and glaciers until it was dark. I tried to go to sleep after it was dark. But I woke up whenever the bus bumped or swayed. We arrived in Edmonton next morning after we had travelled for twenty-six hours. As soon as we stopped, I had a large breakfast. Then I walked around Edmonton which is a large, modern and rather dull city.

The second stage of the journey was from Edmonton to Chicago. This stage was about 2,000 miles and took two days. First, we travelled to Calgary and then southwards until we crossed the frontier into the United States. Then we travelled eastwards across the Prairies until we

UNIT ONE: Composition 2

reached Chicago and the Great Lakes. Chicago is big, busy and interesting.

After I had spent a day in Chicago, I caught another bus to Washington. This third stage took about twelve hours and we travelled through beautiful mountains and woods. I stayed in Washington for two days. While I was staying there, I visited the White House, the Congress, the Lincoln Memorial and the National Space Museum.

The final stage of my journey was from Washington to New York. As soon as I reached New York, I went straight to Kennedy Airport. I wanted to buy a very cheap airline ticket to London. When I arrived at the airport, there was a waiting list for cheap tickets. After I got my name on the list, I went to a student hostel. I stayed in New York for three days and I visited many interesting places, including the Empire State Building and the Statue of Liberty.

UNIT ONE: Composition 2

Preparation and writing

1 **Structure practice**
   a Choose some sentences from the Structure Practice which you will be able to use in your composition.
   b Write them down in the order in which you will use them.

2 **Sample composition**
   a The Sample Composition has six paragraphs. What is each paragraph about?

Example: *Paragraph one — why you made the journey.*
where the journey started and ended.

   b Write down two sentences containing a time clause from each paragraph.

3 **Your writing**
   a Read the subject on page 10.
   b Think about the journey you are going to describe. Decide how many paragraphs you are going to write.
   c Make notes on the contents of each paragraph. Decide when you will use the sentences you have written from the Structure Practice (1b above).
   d You may find it useful to refer to the Sample Composition while you are writing. Make sure you include several sentences containing time clauses in your composition.

4 **Checking your work**
   a Read through your writing carefully.
   b Exchange your work with another student.
   c Check each other's work for any mistakes.

UNIT ONE

Composition **3**

Subject: **Your town or village**

Describe your town or village. Say where it is and write about its houses, shops, industries and public buildings. Write about the different kinds of work people do and how they spend their leisure.

Introducing the subject

Where are you going to write about?
What is . . . like?
Are there any important buildings?
What is the climate like?
What kind of jobs do people in . . . do?
How do people spend their spare time?

Structure practice

Use the sentences below to talk about your town or village. Work in pairs or groups. Try always to say things which are true.

Revision

Time clauses from Compositions One and Two

1 **Ask and answer**
You can answer each question in many different ways.

a | What / Where | do the | young people / older people | of your | town / village | do when there is a public holiday? / go after they finish work?

Example: The young people of my town go to the main square when there is a public holiday.

b | What happens to the people of your | town / village | when they are too old to go to work?

Example: The people of my town get a pension from the Government when they are too old to work.

15

UNIT ONE: Composition 3

c | What do the | boys / girls | of your | town / village | do | when school finishes for the day? / when there is a public holiday? / after they complete their education?

Example: The boys of my town play games, usually football, when school finishes for the day.

New structure
In this composition, you are going to practise sentences containing **because clauses.**

Example: Young people often cannot find work **because there are few jobs available**.

2 Complete
You can complete each sentence in many different ways.

a | Most of the houses ... are | modern / old / built of ... | because ...

Example: Most of the houses in my town are modern because they have been built in the past thirty years.

b People like living in ... part of the town/village because ...

Example: People like living in the new part of the village because the houses are more comfortable.

c | Many / Few | tourists visit ... because ...

Example: Few tourists visit my home town because it is not historical.

d | Most / Many / Some | of the | men / women / young people | get jobs | in factories / on farms / in shops or supermarkets / with the local council / in the public services | because ...

Example: Some of the young people get jobs in shops because there are several large supermarkets.

e The most interesting building in ... is ... because ...

f | Because the climate | is / is not | very | cold in the winter, / hot in the summer, | ...

Example: Because the climate is very cold in winter, people stay at home in the evenings.

3 Ask and answer

You can answer each question in many different ways.

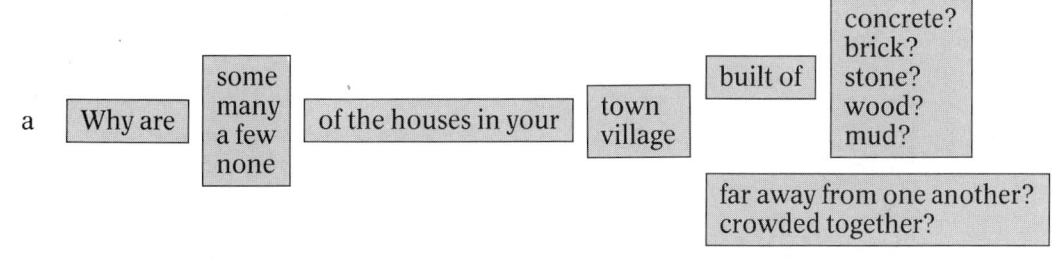

a Why are | some / many / a few / none | of the houses in your | town / village | built of | concrete? / brick? / stone? / wood? / mud? | far away from one another? / crowded together?

Example: Many of the houses in my village are far away from one another because they have large gardens.

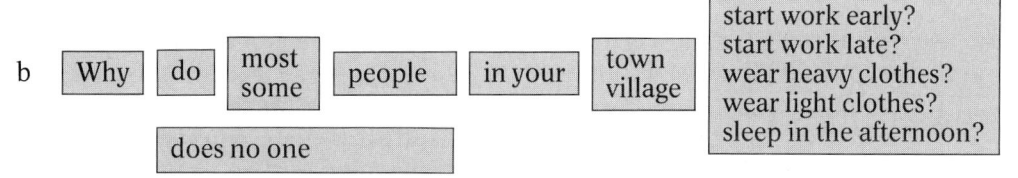

b Why do | most / some | people | in your | town / village | / does no one | start work early? / start work late? / wear heavy clothes? / wear light clothes? / sleep in the afternoon?

Example: Most people in my village start work early because they are farmers.

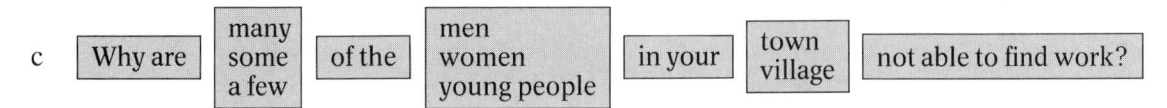

c Why are | many / some / a few | of the | men / women / young people | in your | town / village | not able to find work?

Example: Many young people in my town are not able to find work because many factories have closed.

Sample composition

Read through the following:

Port Glasgow

I live in a town in Scotland called Port Glasgow. The town stands on the River Clyde about twenty miles from the city of Glasgow. Port Glasgow is a small industrial town with a shipyard and other industries.

UNIT ONE: Composition 3

The town is divided into two parts because some of the town is beside the river and some of it is on the hills above the river. The lower part of the town, which is called the town centre, stands beside the river. Most of the houses, flats and shops in the town centre are modern because the old ones were pulled down after the War which ended in 1945. The upper part of the town is also modern because it, also, was built after 1945. The upper part of the town consists of many large housing estates and stands on the hills above the river. There is a shipyard beside the river and a new industrial estate on the hills.

Most of the men work in the shipyard or in the factories on the industrial estate. Some women work in a clothing factory. But many men and women are unemployed because there is not enough work in the shipyard or in the factories on the industrial estate. When young people leave school, they often cannot get work because there are few jobs available. Some young people get jobs in shops, in banks or in public services. Other young people have to leave the town because there is no work for them. Some continue their studies at technical college or at university. But they have to travel outside Port Glasgow because there is no higher education in the town.

In the winter evenings, there is not much for people to do in Port Glasgow after they finish work. Young people can go to youth clubs and other organisations. Older people often stay at home and watch television because it is cold and dark in winter. But there is much more to do in the summer because the evenings are light. In Scotland, the sun does not set until after ten o'clock at night because it is so far north. Young people can play football or other games on the large playing fields near the town. Older people can go walking on the hills or sit in the park beside the river.

UNIT ONE: Composition 3

Preparation and writing

1 **Structure practice**
   a Choose some sentences from the Structure Practice which you will be able to use in your composition.
   b Write them down in the order in which you will use them.

2 **Sample composition**
   a The Sample Composition has four paragraphs. What is each paragraph about?

Example: *Paragraph One – Port Glasgow, where it is and what it's like.*

   b Write down two sentences containing a *because* clause from paragraphs 2, 3 and 4.

3 **Your writing**
   a Read the subject on page 15.
   b Think about the town or village you are going to write about. Decide how many paragraphs you are going to write.
   c Make short notes on the contents of each paragraph. Decide when you will use the sentences you have written from the Structure Practice (1b above).
   d You may find it useful to refer to the Sample Composition while you are writing. Make sure you use several sentences containing *because* clauses in your composition.

4 **Checking your work**
   a Read through your writing carefully.
   b Exchange your work with another student.
   c Check each other's work for any mistakes.

19

UNIT ONE
Composition 4

Subject: **A wedding**

Write about the wedding of a relation or a friend which you went to. Say how the bride and bridegroom met and where the wedding took place. Describe the whole of the wedding day or days. First describe the marriage ceremony. Then write about the celebrations describing the food, the music and so on. If you are married, you may describe your own wedding.

UNIT ONE: Composition 4

Introducing the subject

Have you ever been to a wedding?
What was the last wedding you went to?
Where did the wedding take place?
Were there many guests?
What happened at the wedding party?

Structure practice

Use the sentences below to talk about a wedding of a relation or friend you went to. Work in pairs or groups. Try always to say things which really happened.

Revision

Time clauses from Compositions One and Two

1 Ask and answer
You can answer each question in many different ways.

> What happened
>
> before the bride arrived?
> as soon as the marriage ceremony was finished?
> when the guests arrived at the house?
> after the guests had finished eating?

Example: As soon as the marriage ceremony was finished, all the guests came to our house.

Revision

Because clauses from Composition Three

2 Ask and answer
You can answer each question in many different ways.

> Why did you go to the wedding?
> Why did the wedding take place on . . . ?
> Why was the marriage ceremony held in . . . ?
> Why did some people travel a long way to the wedding?

Example: The wedding took place on a Saturday because Saturday is a holiday for most people.

21

UNIT ONE: Composition 4

New structure

In this composition, you are going to practise sentences containing **adjectival clauses** (relative clauses).

Examples: My sister, **who is twenty-three years old**, got married this summer.
The dress **she wore** was made of white silk.

3 Complete
You can complete each sentence in many different ways.

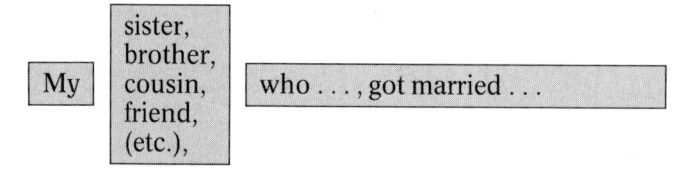

| My | sister, brother, cousin, friend, (etc.), | who ..., got married ... |

The wedding took place at/in ..., which is ...
The dress the bride wore was made of ...
The relations who ... stayed ...
The rings the couple gave each other ...
There was lots of food which had been prepared by ...

Example: The wedding took place in Cornwall, which is in the West of England.

4 Complete
You can complete each sentence in many different ways.

a | The presents / The food / The flowers | they were given ... / her mother prepared ... / some relatives brought ... |

Example: The flowers some relatives brought looked beautiful.

b | The marriage ceremony, / The reception, / The party, / The dancing, / The singing, / The celebrations, / The meal, / (etc.) | which lasted for ..., | was ... / consisted of ... |

Example: The marriage ceremony, which lasted for one hour, consisted of prayers and singing.

22

5 Ask and answer
You can answer each question in many different ways.

| What did | your relatives / the bride's parents / you | do for the guests | who arrived early? / who stayed late? |

Example: My relatives offered tea to the guests who arrived early.

6 Tell each other

| Describe | the food you were given. / the other guests who were invited. / the presents the couple were given. / the music that was played. / the present you gave them. |

Example: The other guests who were invited were relatives and friends of both families.

Sample composition

Read through the following:

My sister's wedding

My sister, who is twenty-three years old, got married this summer. She met her husband while they were both studying at the same university. They got married at our home, which is in Cornwall in the West of England. Her husband's family stayed with my parents for the wedding because they live in another part of England.

The wedding took place on a Saturday, which is the usual day for weddings in England, because Saturday is a holiday for most people. The wedding, which lasted for most of the day, consisted of three parts. First, there was the marriage ceremony, which started at 12 noon and lasted for about an hour. Then, there was the wedding reception, which lasted all the afternoon. And, finally, after the couple had left for their honeymoon, there was a party which went on all evening.

UNIT ONE: Composition 4

> The marriage ceremony took place in the local church, which is a beautiful old building. The relatives of both families, who had travelled a long way, filled the church because it is only small. After all the guests had arrived at the church, my sister arrived. The dress she wore was made of white silk and she looked lovely. The most important part of the ceremony is the vows which the priest reads and the couple repeats. Then they gave each other rings, which were made of gold. Finally, the couple signed a certificate which is the legal evidence of their marriage. As soon as the marriage was finished, people took lots of photographs outside the church.
>
> As soon as the photographs were taken, the guests all came to our house for the wedding reception. The reception was held in the garden, which looks very pretty in the summer. There was lots of delicious food which had been prepared by friends and family. Everyone enjoyed themselves, eating, talking and meeting people. Finally, the wedding cake was cut, which everyone has to taste at a wedding, and speeches were made about the couple and the wedding. The presents they had been given were displayed in the house because people like seeing everything. They had been mainly given things which would be useful in their home.
>
> At the end of the afternoon, the couple changed into different clothes, which were for travelling. When the couple left at the end of the afternoon, everyone tied things onto their car and threw rice and confetti at them. Then we all continued to enjoy ourselves for the rest of the day.

Preparation and writing

1. **Structure practice**
   a. Choose some sentences from the Structure Practice which you will be able to use in your composition.
   b. Write them down in the order in which you will use them.

2. **Sample composition**
   a. The Sample Composition has three paragraphs. What is each paragraph about?

Example: *Paragraph One – general introduction: who got married, when, where, etc.*

   b. Write down two sentences containing adjectival clauses from paragraphs 1, 2, 3 and 4.

3 **Your writing**
   a Read the subject on page 20.
   b Think about the wedding you are going to describe. Decide how many paragraphs you are going to write.
   c Make notes on the contents of each paragraph. Decide when you will use the sentences you have written from the Structure Practice (1b above).
   d You may find it useful to refer to the Sample Composition while you are writing. Make sure you include several sentences containing adjectival clauses in your composition.

4 **Checking your work**
   a Read through your writing carefully.
   b Exchange your work with another student.
   c Check each other's work for any mistakes.

UNIT ONE
Composition 5

Subject: **Lost and found**

Tell the story of an occasion when you lost something. Explain in detail how you lost it and how you tried to find it again.

Introducing the subject

Can you remember ever losing anything?
Do you often lose things?
What is the most important thing you have ever lost?
Where did you lose it?
How did you try to find it?
Did you find it?

Structure practice

Use the sentences and questions below to talk about an occasion when you lost something. Work in pairs or groups. Try always to say things which really happened.

Revision

Because clauses from Composition Three

1 **Ask and answer**
   You can answer each question in many different ways.

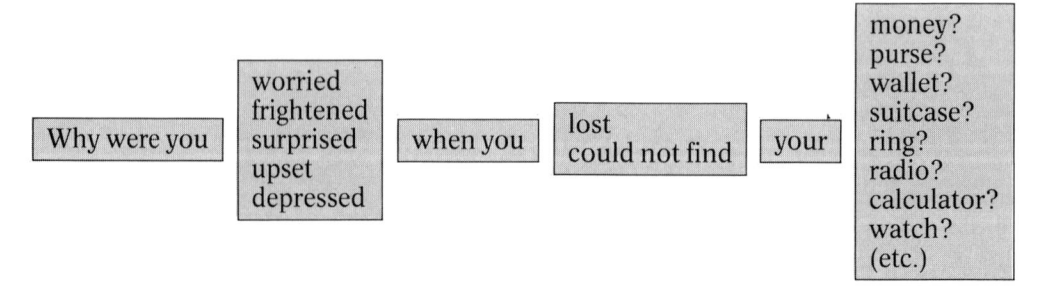

| Why were you | worried / frightened / surprised / upset / depressed | when you | lost / could not find | your | money? / purse? / wallet? / suitcase? / ring? / radio? / calculator? / watch? / (etc.) |

Example: I was very worried when I lost my briefcase because it contained some important papers.

26

2 **Complete**
You can complete each sentence in many different ways.

I lost my . . . because I was . . .

Example: I lost my suitcase because I was in a great hurry.

3 **Ask and answer**
You can answer each question in many different ways.

| Why did you | telephone . . . ?
go back to . . . ?
ask Y to . . . ? (*Y is the name of a person*)
write a letter to . . . ? |

Example: I telephoned the cinema because I might have dropped my purse there.

New structure

In this composition, you are going to practise sentences containing **adjectival clauses** again (as in Composition Four). In this composition, you are going to practise some **adjectival clauses** beginning with **where**.

Example: I ran back to the station **where I had just got off the train**.

4 **Complete**
You can complete each sentence in many different ways.

a
The X I had lost . . . *(X is something you lost)*
I went back to the place where . . .
The man who . . . had not seen my X.
I could not remember the time at which I had . . .
Everybody tried to help me, which . . .

Example: The watch I had lost was a birthday present from my father.

b The | bus / train / boat / taxi | I was travelling on/in . . .
I caught . . .
I left my X on/in . . .

Example: The train I caught was very crowded.

27

c The [shopkeeper / man / woman / official / policeman (etc.)] who had ... [did not recognise me again. / was not helpful.]

Example: The official who had been on duty did not recognise me again.

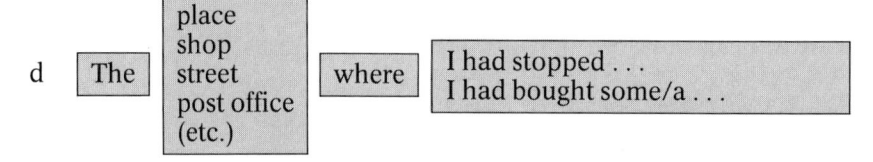

d The [place / shop / street / post office (etc.)] where [I had stopped ... / I had bought some/a ...]

Example: The shop where I had bought a magazine was closed.

Sample composition

Read through the following:

How I lost and found my suitcase

This is the story of an occasion when I lost a suitcase on a railway train. I was very worried when I lost my suitcase because it contained some important papers for my work.

One evening, I left my office in Central London at about 6 o'clock. I did not go home because I had to go to a meeting in South London. I was carrying my briefcase and a small blue suitcase. I walked to London Bridge Station and I caught a train which runs between London Bridge Station and Victoria Station. The 6.15 train I caught was very crowded. The small station where I got off was two stations from London Bridge. I was in a great hurry because I was late.

I walked quickly out of the station and towards the place where I was going. After I had walked for a few minutes, I suddenly realised that I had left my small blue suitcase on the train! Immediately, I ran back to the station. I asked the porter who was on duty at the station to telephone Victoria Station, where the train was going. But the porter, who was not very helpful, said there was no telephone in the station. So I got on the next train which was going to Victoria.

UNIT ONE: Composition 5

When I reached Victoria Station, I went straight to the Lost Property Office. But the suitcase I had lost had not been found. The original train in which I had been travelling had now gone back to London Bridge Station. The Lost Property man could not telephone London Bridge Station because he was very busy. I was very worried because the suitcase I had lost contained important papers which I needed the next day. So I went to the Station Manager's office.

The Station Manager, who was very helpful, telephoned all the stations where the train had stopped, but my suitcase had not been found. Finally, he telephoned London Bridge, but it had not been found there either. Perhaps my suitcase was still on the original train. This train was about to arrive at Victoria Station again! Because I was determined to find my suitcase, I went and searched the train and I spoke to the guard. But I could not find my suitcase. Finally, I went back to the Station Manager. I gave him my telephone number and asked to be phoned if my suitcase was found.

While I was travelling home, I felt very depressed because I had wasted the whole evening looking unsuccessfully for my suitcase. As soon as I arrived home, the telephone rang. It was the Station Manager's Office at Victoria Station. They were telephoning because they had just found my suitcase.

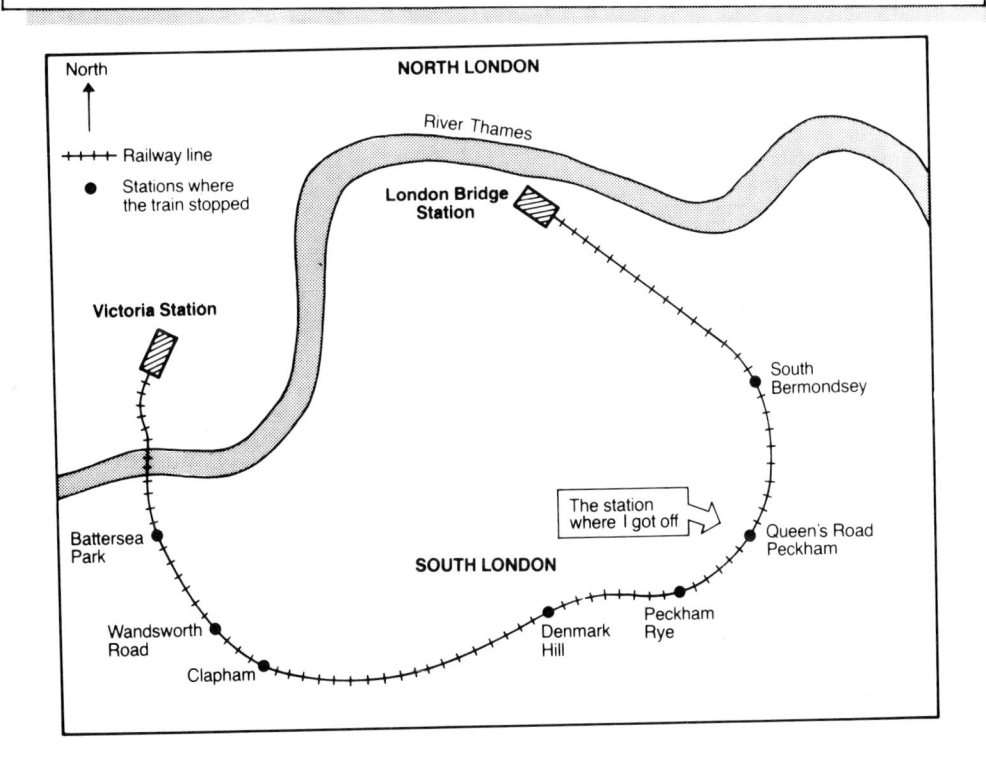

UNIT ONE: Composition 5

Preparation and writing

1   Structure practice
   a   Choose some sentences from the Structure Practice which you will be able to use in your composition.
   b   Write them down in the order in which you will use them.

2   Sample composition
   a   The Sample Composition has six paragraphs. What is each paragraph about?

Example: *Paragraph One – Introduction – what was lost and why it was important.*

   b   Write down two sentences containing adjectival clauses from paragraphs 2, 3 and 4.

3   Your writing
   a   Read the subject on page 26.
   b   Think about an occasion when you lost something. Decide how many paragraphs you are going to write.
   c   Make notes on the contents of each paragraph. Decide when you will use the sentences you have written from the Structure Practice (1b above).
   d   You may find it useful to refer to the Sample Composition while you are writing. Make sure you include several sentences containing adjectival clauses beginning with where in your composition.

4   Checking your work
   a   Read through your writing carefully.
   b   Exchange your work with another student.
   c   Check each other's work for any mistakes.

UNIT ONE

Composition

6

Planning and writing a free composition

Planning

1 Content and language
After you have read the *subject* for your composition, begin to think about the *content* of your composition – ie. what you can write about. At the same time, think about the *language* you will use in your writing – the vocabulary and structures. This first stage of preparation for Composition One is shown in the example. *Structure Practice* for each guided composition helps with this first stage of planning.

Example:

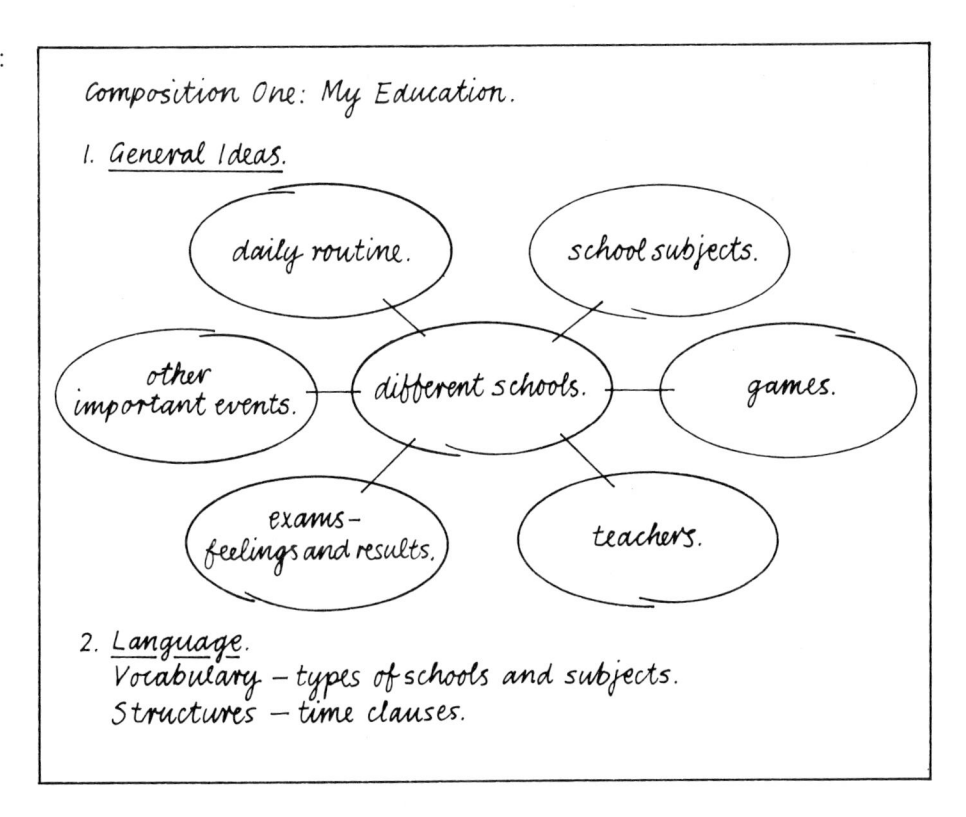

```
Composition One: My Education.

1. General Ideas.

    daily routine.        school subjects.

  other
  important events. — different schools. — games.

       exams -
    feelings and results.      teachers.

2. Language.
    Vocabulary – types of schools and subjects.
    Structures – time clauses.
```

Exercise 1
Make notes as in the example for (a) content and (b) language for either Composition Two *or* Four. Make notes for either your own composition or for the Sample Composition.

31

UNIT ONE: Composition 6

2 Sequencing

Before you write your composition, you have to decide upon the order or *sequence* of the content.

Chronological order

Look at the example for Sample Composition One. What is the sequence based upon? It is based on chronological order – the order in which the events happened in time. This is the simplest and often the best way of planning the sequence of the content of your composition.

Example:

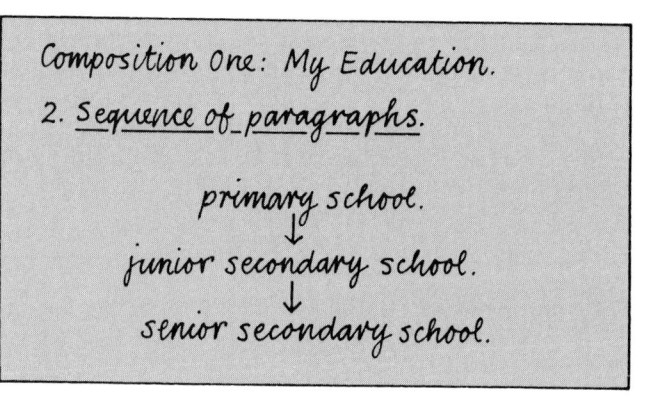

> Composition One: My Education.
> 2. Sequence of paragraphs.
>
> primary school.
> ↓
> junior secondary school.
> ↓
> senior secondary school.

Exercise 2

For each Sample Composition, you have made notes of the content of each paragraph. Look again at your notes for Sample Compositions Two, Four and Five. What is the sequence of the paragraphs? Do your own compositions follow the same sequence or a different sequence?

Series of topics

Not all compositions can be sequenced in chronological order. Look at the example for Sample Composition Three. What is the sequence based upon? It is based on a series of topics related to the general subject.

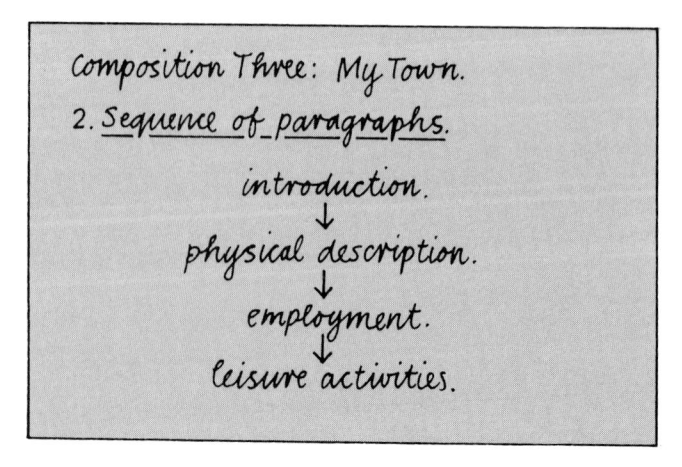

Example:

> Composition Three: My Town.
> 2. Sequence of paragraphs.
>
> introduction.
> ↓
> physical description.
> ↓
> employment.
> ↓
> leisure activities.

Exercise 3
Read your own Composition Three. What is the sequence of the content?

Your writing

Choose *one* of the following subjects for your composition.

1. Tell the story of how you tried to help a friend who got into difficulties. Explain what the difficulty was and how you tried to help. Say whether or not you succeeded.

2. Write about an important event which took place recently in your family or among your friends.

3. Tell the story of an ordinary day in the life of a relative or a friend.

Before you begin planning your composition, look back at the Structure Practices for Compositions One to Five.

First, write down your general ideas for (a) content and (b) language. Make notes like the ones in the example for Composition One.

Second, decide on the sequence for your composition. Make notes of the sequence of paragraphs. Decide first whether the sequence will be in chronological order or in a series of topics.

Third, write two or three sentences that you may use in each paragraph. Try to write some sentences containing time clauses, *because* clauses and adjectival clauses.

Fourth, write the first draft of your composition.

Fifth, read your draft composition, correct it and improve it.

Sixth, make a final copy of your composition.

UNIT TWO

Composition 7

Subject: **Wanting money for something**

Tell the story of how you needed to get money for something. Say what you wanted the money for and how you tried to get the money. Say whether you succeeded in the end or not.

Introducing the subject

Can you think of an occasion when you needed money for something?
Why didn't you have enough money?
How much did you need?
Could you borrow the money?
What did you do?

Structure practice

Revision

Adjectival clauses from Composition Four and Five

1 **Complete**

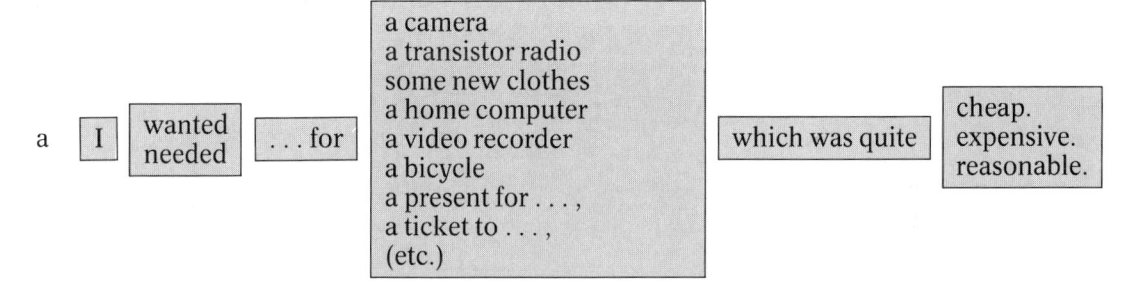

a   I [wanted / needed] ... for [a camera / a transistor radio / some new clothes / a home computer / a video recorder / a bicycle / a present for ..., / a ticket to ..., / (etc.)] which was quite [cheap. / expensive. / reasonable.]

Examples: I wanted £80 for a bicycle, which was quite reasonable.
I needed £12 for the bus fare to the capital, which was quite expensive.

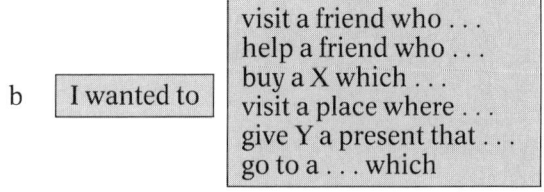

b   I wanted to [visit a friend who ... / help a friend who ... / buy a X which ... / visit a place where ... / give Y a present that ... / go to a ... which]

(X is something)   (Y is the name of a person)

Example: I wanted to go to a football match which cost £10.

c   I had to think of a way by which ...

d   I [saved up / earned / borrowed] the money that ...

Example: I earned all the money that I needed.

35

UNIT TWO: Composition 7

New structure

In this composition, you are going to practise sentences containing **so that clauses**.

Examples: I decided to find a job in the evenings **so that I could earn enough money to buy a second-hand cassette deck.**
I stopped spending money on sweets **so that I would be able to save up for my holiday.**

Note: The modal verbs **could** and **would** are often used in **so that clauses**.

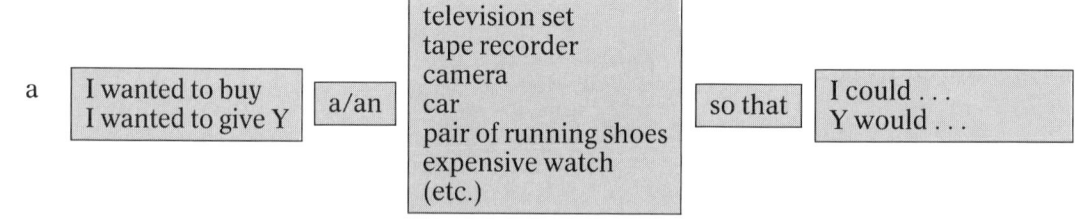

2 Complete

a | I wanted to buy / I wanted to give Y | a/an | television set / tape recorder / camera / car / pair of running shoes / expensive watch / (etc.) | so that | I could ... / Y would ...

Examples: I wanted to buy a bicycle so that I could ride to school everyday.
I wanted to give my brother an expensive watch so that he would have a special birthday present.

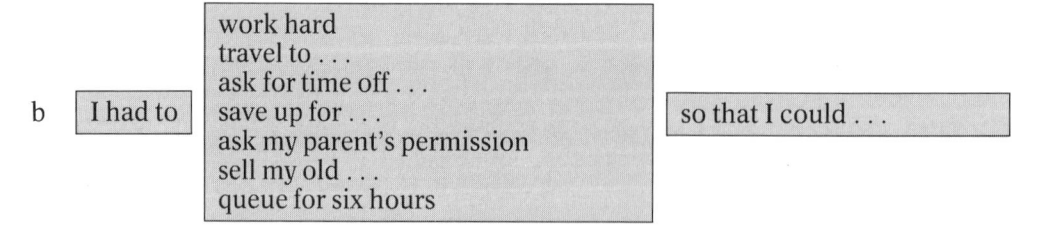

b | I had to | work hard / travel to ... / ask for time off ... / save up for ... / ask my parent's permission / sell my old ... / queue for six hours | so that I could ...

Example: I had to sell my old radio so that I could get the rest of the money.

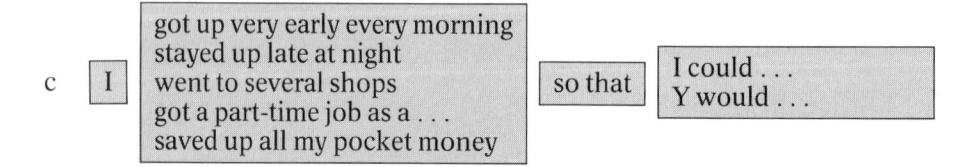

c | I | got up very early every morning / stayed up late at night / went to several shops / got a part-time job as a ... / saved up all my pocket money | so that | I could ... / Y would ...

Example: I got up early every morning so that I could do a job and earn the money I needed.

Note: The question: Why did Tom get up early every morning?
can be answered in two different ways:

(i) Tom got up early every morning **because** he had to do an hour's work before school.

(ii) Tom got up early every morning **so that** he could do an hour's work before school.

3 **Ask and answer**
Ask one another the following questions and give one answer using **because** and one answer using **so that**.

a Why did you want to buy a/an . . .?
b Why did your father give you ten pounds?
c Why did you have to save up?

Sample composition

Read through the following:

Money for a bicycle

When I first went to secondary school, most of the other children in my class had bicycles. Many of the children who had bicycles were friends of mine. I felt jealous because I did not have a bicycle. My friends used to ride together in the evenings to the river which was about seven miles away. I wanted to have a bicycle so that I could go with them. I also wanted a bicycle so that I could ride to school. Because my school was more than five miles from my house, I had to take a bus there and back every day.

After I had been at secondary school for three weeks, one of the boys wanted to sell his bicycle because he had been given a new one. He was ready to sell it for sixty pounds, which was quite cheap. I asked my father to give me sixty pounds so that I could buy the bicycle. But my father, who did not have much money, was unwilling to spend so much money on something which he considered a luxury. I pointed out that if I rode to school I would not have to spend so much money on bus fares. After a lot of discussion, he agreed to give me half the money I needed. I had to find a part-time job so that I could get the rest of the money. Luckily, the boy agreed not to sell the bicycle for two months.

I thought about it for a few days. Then I had an idea. Many of our neighbours had cars. Perhaps they would pay me to wash the cars for them. I borrowed a bucket and a large sponge from my mother so that I could clean the cars properly. On Saturday morning, I got up early so that I would find people at home. I went to a neighbour's house and asked her

UNIT TWO: Composition 7

> if she wanted to have her car washed. She was very pleased and offered to pay me one pound. I worked very hard so that the car would look really clean. It took me more than an hour to wash the car. On that first Saturday, I earned three pounds. I had to spend every Saturday for the next eight weeks so that I could earn the money I needed.
>
> My father was very pleased when I showed him the money. He gave me the other thirty pounds so that I could buy the bicycle. On Monday morning, I went to school very early so that I could find the boy who wanted to sell his bicycle. He had kept his promise and had not sold the bicycle to anyone else. He agreed to bring the bicycle to my house that evening. You can imagine how happy I felt while I was riding to school the following morning on my new bicycle. Also, you can imagine my feelings when I rode with my friends to the river in the evening.

Preparation and writing

1 **Structure practice**
   a Choose some sentences from the Structure Practice which you will be able to use in your composition.
   b Write them down in the order in which you will use them.

2 **Sample composition**
   a The Sample Composition has four paragraphs. What is each paragraph about?

Example: Paragraph One – what the writer wanted.
– why the writer wanted a bicycle.

   b Write down two sentences containing *so that* clauses from paragraphs 1, 2, 3 and 4.

3 **Your writing**
   a Read the subject on page 34.
   b Think about something you very much wanted to get. How did you go about getting it? Decide how many paragraphs you are going to write.
   c Make notes on the contents of each paragraph. Decide when you will use the sentences you have written from the Structure Practice (1b above).
   d You may find it useful to refer to the Sample Composition while you are writing. Make sure you include several sentences containing *so that* clauses in your composition.

4 **Checking your work**
   a Read through your writing carefully.
   b Exchange your work with another student.
   c Check each other's work for any mistakes.

UNIT TWO

Composition 8

Subject: **An important interview, examination or meeting**

Write about a very important examination, interview or meeting which you once took part in. Carefully describe how you prepared for it, what happened at each stage and what happened afterwards. Also describe the feelings and thoughts you experienced at each stage.

Introducing the subject

Have you ever been to a very important interview or meeting?
Why was it important?
How did you feel before it started?
What happened?
What is the most important examination you have ever taken?
How many papers and subjects did you have to take?
How did you feel after the examination?

Structure practice

Revision

so that clauses from Composition Seven

1 **Complete**

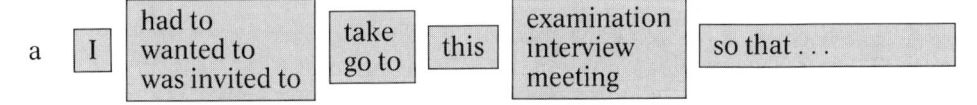

a I | had to / wanted to / was invited to | take / go to | this | examination / interview / meeting | so that ...

Example: I had to go to this meeting so that I could disagree with the plan for an airport.

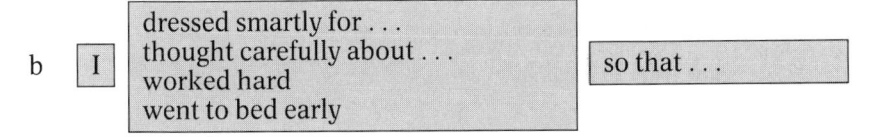

b I | dressed smartly for ... / thought carefully about ... / worked hard / went to bed early | so that ...

Example: I thought carefully about my speech so that people would agree with my point of view.

39

Revision
Adjectival clauses from Composition Four and Five

2 Complete

a │ The place where the │ meeting / interview / examination │ was held was . . .

Example: The place where the meeting was held was a large hall in the centre of the town.

b │ The │ interview, examination, meeting, │ which lasted for . . . , consisted of . . .

Example: The meeting, which lasted for three hours, consisted of members of the public making speeches for or against the new airport.

c The questions I was asked . . .

Example: The questions I was asked were difficult.

New structure

In this composition, you are going to practise sentences containing **noun clauses** which begin with the word **that** or with no introductory word. We shall call these **noun clauses (statements)**.

Examples: The teacher warned me **that the examination would be very difficult**.
I was sure **I would not pass the examination**.

Note: In **noun clauses** the auxiliary verb **would** is often used.

Examples: The teacher said, 'The examination **will** be very difficult.'
The teacher warned me that the examination **would** be very difficult.

3 Complete

a │ A friend / A student / A teacher │ who had passed / who had failed / who knew all about / who had attended │ a similar / the same │ examination / interview / meeting │ said . . . / suggested . . . / explained . . . / advised . . .

Example: A friend who had failed a similar interview advised that I should prepare for it very carefully.

b │ A friend / A teacher / Y / I │ warned / reminded / promised / informed │ Y / me / him / her / my . . . │ that . . . *(Y is the name of a person)*

Example: I promised my parents that I would work as hard as possible.

UNIT TWO: Composition 8

4 Ask and answer

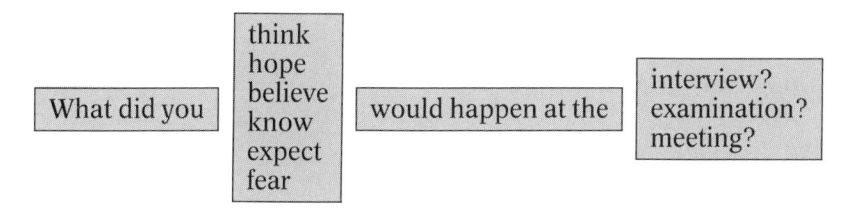

What did you | think / hope / believe / know / expect / fear | would happen at the | interview? / examination? / meeting?

Example: I hoped that the members of the committee would agree with my plans at the meeting.

5 Ask and complete

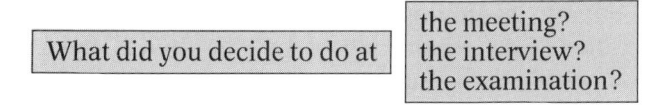

What did you decide to do at | the meeting? / the interview? / the examination?

I decided that I would . . .

6 Complete

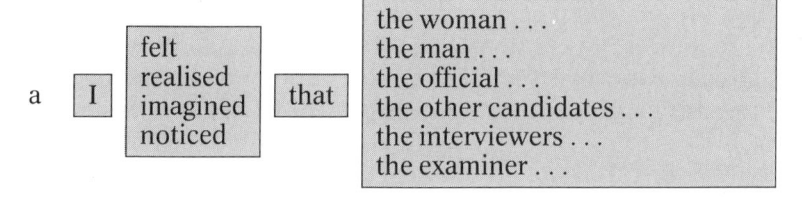

a   I | felt / realised / imagined / noticed | that | the woman . . . / the man . . . / the official . . . / the other candidates . . . / the interviewers . . . / the examiner . . .

Example: I realised that the interviewers wanted me to feel relaxed.

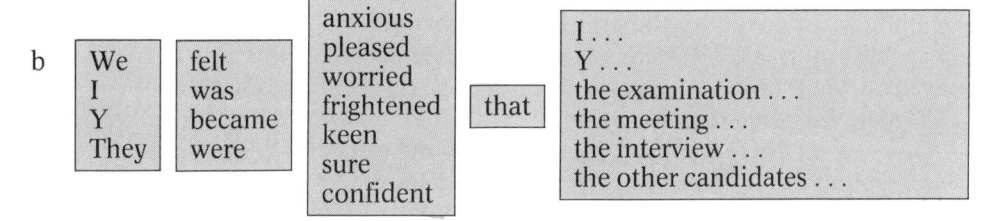

b   We / I / Y / They | felt / was / became / were | anxious / pleased / worried / frightened / keen / sure / confident | that | I . . . / Y . . . / the examination . . . / the meeting . . . / the interview . . . / the other candidates . . .

Example: I felt confident that I had impressed the interviewers.

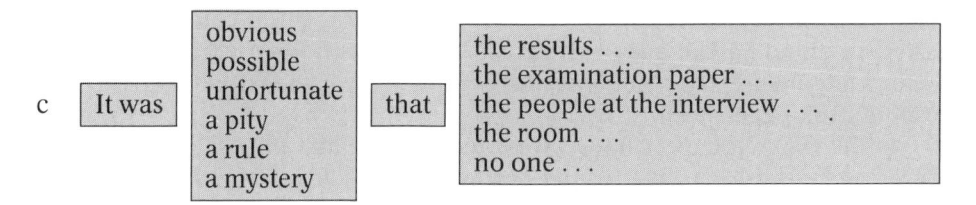

c   It was | obvious / possible / unfortunate / a pity / a rule / a mystery | that | the results . . . / the examination paper . . . / the people at the interview . . . / the room . . . / no one . . .

Example: It was unfortunate that the results were delayed by two months.

41

Sample composition

Read through the following:

An examination and an interview

I am going to write about an examination and an interview which I had to take so that I could go to university. When I was in my last year at school, I decided that I wanted to study English at the University of Cambridge. But I knew that there was a special examination and interview for Cambridge. The examination, which lasted for three days, consisted of five examination papers and an interview. My English teacher, who knew all about the examination, warned me that it would be very difficult. She suggested that I should give up the other things that I was doing so that I could spend all my time preparing for the examination. It was a pity I had to give up my jazz group, but I agreed. I promised her I would work as hard as possible.

In December, I went to Cambridge for three days. I travelled to Cambridge by train the day before the examination. When I reached Cambridge, I went to the college where the examination was to take place. I was given a room which belonged to a university student who was on holiday. The room was full of interesting things. As I sat in the room, I felt that I was already a university student myself. Then I remembered that I had not passed my entrance examination yet – I had not even taken it.

At dinner that evening, I chatted to some of the other young people who had come to take the entrance examination. I am sure we all felt very anxious, but we all pretended we were not worried about the examination. That evening, as I went to bed, I felt sure the other candidates were better than me and that I would not pass the examination.

Next morning, I did not eat any breakfast because I felt very nervous. I went straight to the examination room so that I would not be late. I thought the first two papers were very difficult and I doubted I would pass. I felt sure that the other candidates had done better than me. On the second day, I had my interview with a lecturer. I was very anxious that the lecturer would ask me questions which I could not answer. But, as soon as I went into the room, I realised he was very friendly. He suggested I tell him about the poets I was interested in. It was obvious that he wanted me to feel relaxed. We had a very interesting discussion which lasted for about half an hour. Afterwards, I felt confident that I had done well. I felt much more confident that I could answer the remaining two examination papers well.

At the end of the three days, I was very pleased that the examinations were finished. I hoped the results would come quickly so that I could stop worrying. Two weeks later, I received a letter which informed me that I had passed and that I could study at Cambridge.

Preparation and writing

1 **Structure practice**
   a Choose some sentences from the Structure Practice which you will be able to use in your composition.
   b Write them down in the order in which you will use them.

2 **Sample composition**
   a The Sample Composition has five paragraphs. What is each paragraph about?

Example: *Paragraph One — subject of composition.*
   — reasons for taking the examination.
   — what it consisted of.
   — preparing for it.

   b Write down three sentences containing a noun clause (statement) from paragraphs 1, 3 and 4.

3 **Your writing**
   a Read the subject on page 39.
   b Think about a very important examination, interview or meeting which you took part in. Decide how many paragraphs you are going to write.
   c Make notes on the contents of each paragraph. Decide when you will use the sentences you have written from the Structure Practice (1b above).
   d You may find it useful to refer to the Sample Composition while you are writing. Make sure you include several sentences containing a noun clause (statement) in your composition.

4 **Checking your work**
   a Read through your writing carefully.
   b Exchange your work with another student.
   c Check each other's work for any mistakes.

UNIT TWO

Composition 9

Subject: **A theft**

Tell the story of how something belonging to you was stolen. Say what was stolen and how it was stolen. Say who you thought the thief was and explain why. Say whether or not you got the thing back.

UNIT TWO: Composition 9

Introducing the subject

Do you ever hear about thefts or robberies?
What kind of things are stolen?
How are they stolen?
Has anyone heard of a robbery recently?
Have you ever had anything stolen?
How do you know it was stolen?
What did you do?

Structure practice

Revision

Noun clauses (statements) from Composition 8

1 Complete

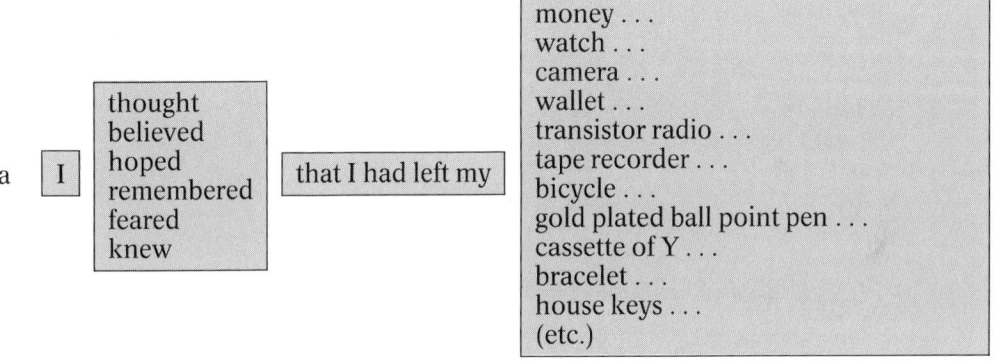

a | I | → | thought / believed / hoped / remembered / feared / knew | → | that I had left my | → | money... / watch... / camera... / wallet... / transistor radio... / tape recorder... / bicycle... / gold plated ball point pen... / cassette of Y... / bracelet... / house keys... / (etc.) |

(Y is your favourite singer)

Example: I thought that I had left my camera in my bedroom.

b I thought that my X, which ..., had been ...

Example: I thought that my camera, which was expensive, had been stolen.

c I remembered I had seen a person who ...

Example: I remembered I had seen a person who looked suspicious.

New structure

In this composition, you are going to practise sentences containing **noun clauses (questions)** introduced by **where, who, when, why, how, what,** and **if**.

Examples: I did not know **where I had left my camera**.
I asked my brother **if he had seen my watch**.
I wondered **if I had left it at the place where we had the picnic**.

45

UNIT TWO: Composition 9

We shall call these clauses **noun clauses (questions)**.

Note: I asked my brother, '**Have** you **seen** my watch?'
I told my father, 'I **lost** my watch yesterday.'
I asked my brother if **he had seen** my watch.
I told my father I **had lost** my watch.

2 Complete
I did not know where I had ... my X. (*X is a thing*)
When I told a friend that I had lost my X, he asked me who ...
I tried to remember where ...
There were no holes in my pockets, so I wondered how ...
When I went to the police-station, a policeman asked me why ...
I went to the railway-station and I asked an official if anyone had ...
I could not think what had ...
When I woke up, I realised what was ...

Example: I went to the railway station and asked an official if anyone had handed in my suitcase.

3 Complete
Use verbs and verbal phrases such as:

| wondered | could not think | tried to remember |
| find out | asked myself | decided to |

You will find other examples of these verbs and verbal phrases in 2, 3b, 3c and 3d.

a I ...
   where my X could be.
   who had taken my X.
   when I had last seen my X.
   why I had not noticed sooner that it was missing.
   how my friend had deceived me.
   what I could do next.
   if I had dropped my X somewhere.

Example: I tried to remember where I had been when I had last used the camera.

b You wondered what had happened to your X and you tried to think of ways of finding it.

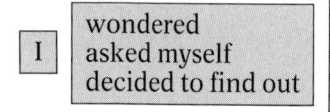

I wondered
   asked myself
   decided to find out

   if ...
   who ...
   where ...
   when ...

Example: I wondered if I should go to the police.

46

UNIT TWO: Composition 9

c   A friend tried to help you.

| A friend | discovered
knew
suggested
asked | how . . .
what . . .
when . . .
where . . .
who . . . |

Example: A friend suggested how my camera had been stolen.

d   You accused someone of taking your X.

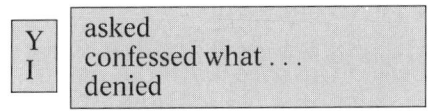

| Y
I | asked
confessed what . . .
denied |

(Y is the name of a person)

Example: Peter confessed what he had done.

Sample composition

Read through the following:

How my gold watch was stolen

When I was at university, I did not have very much money. I could not afford expensive things like a camera. But I did have one thing which was valuable. It was a gold watch, which was a gift from my parents for my twenty-first birthday. And I made the bad mistake of taking it with me on a holiday abroad. I wondered at the time if I was doing the right thing. Now I know what a fool I was.

At the end of the first year, I was wondering what I was going to do during the summer holidays. Then I received a letter from Peter. Peter was a friend who was working for the British Council in Germany. In his letter, Peter asked me if I would come and stay with him for the summer. I decided to accept his invitation. I travelled cheaply to Germany from London by train and by boat. I did not have anything of value with me except my watch which was on my wrist. During the long journey, I often wondered what the time was and I kept looking at my watch.

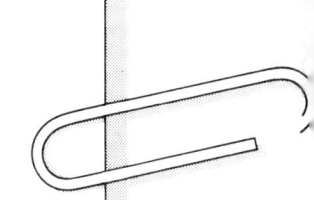

UNIT TWO: Composition 9

> When I arrived in Bonn, where Peter worked, he was waiting for me at the bus station. He took me in his car to his small flat, which was in a quiet side street. At the front, the flat was high off the ground. But, at the back, the bedroom windows were at ground level. It was the month of July and the flat was very hot. I wondered if I would be able to sleep in such heat. I asked Peter if I should keep the bedroom windows open. Peter advised me to keep the windows closed. He said that a stranger had been seen in the neighbourhood at night. The neighbours wondered if the stranger was a thief.
>
> In the evening, we had a wonderful meal in a little restaurant. When we got back to the flat, I felt very hot and tired. I went to bed and soon fell asleep. But before long I was wide awake. It was too hot and I could not sleep. I asked myself what I could do. Then I had an idea. I put my clothes and everything in my bag, including my precious watch, tied the top tightly and laid it at the foot of the bed. I was sure that a thief could not reach it because it was so far away from the windows. Then I opened the windows and fell fast asleep.
>
> Later in the night, I suddenly woke up. Something was moving in the bedroom. I looked round and realised what was happening. There was a thief outside the window. He was holding a long piece of metal with a hook on one end. He had caught my bag with this hook and he was lifting it off the bed and was pulling it towards the window. I jumped up quickly and shouted loudly. But it was too late. The thief had run off with my canvas bag. And my precious watch was inside it. I realised what a fool I had been.

Preparation and writing

1 **Structure practice**
   a Choose some sentences from the Structure Practice which you will be able to use in your composition.
   b Write them down in the order in which you will use them.

2 **Sample composition**
   a The Sample Composition has five paragraphs. What is each paragraph about?

Example: *Paragraph One – the writer made a mistake when he took an expensive wrist watch with him on holiday.*

   b Write down a sentence containing a noun clause (question) from paragraphs 1, 2, 3, 4 and 5.

3 Your writing
   a Read the subject on page 44.
   b Think about an occasion when something belonging to you was stolen. Decide how many paragraphs you are going to write.
   c Make notes on the contents of each paragraph. Decide when you will use the sentences you have written from the Structure Practice (1b above).
   d You may find it useful to refer to the Sample Composition while you are writing. Make sure you include several sentences containing a noun clause (question) in your composition.

4 Checking your work
   a Read through your writing carefully.
   b Exchange your work with another student.
   c Check each other's work for any mistakes.

UNIT TWO
Composition
10

Subject: **An imaginary holiday**

If someone offered to pay all your expenses for a month's holiday anywhere in the world, where would you go and what would you do? Discuss the different places you might like to visit. Choose where you would go and explain why. Then describe what you would do on your holiday.

UNIT TWO: Composition 10

Introducing the subject

Why is it difficult to go abroad?
Has anyone visited any foreign countries?
Have you got any relations or friends who live abroad?
What countries do you think would be the most enjoyable to visit and why?
What countries would be the most interesting to visit and why?

Structure practice

Revision

Noun clauses from Compositions Eight and Nine

1 Complete
a I think I would like to visit . . . and . . . and . . .

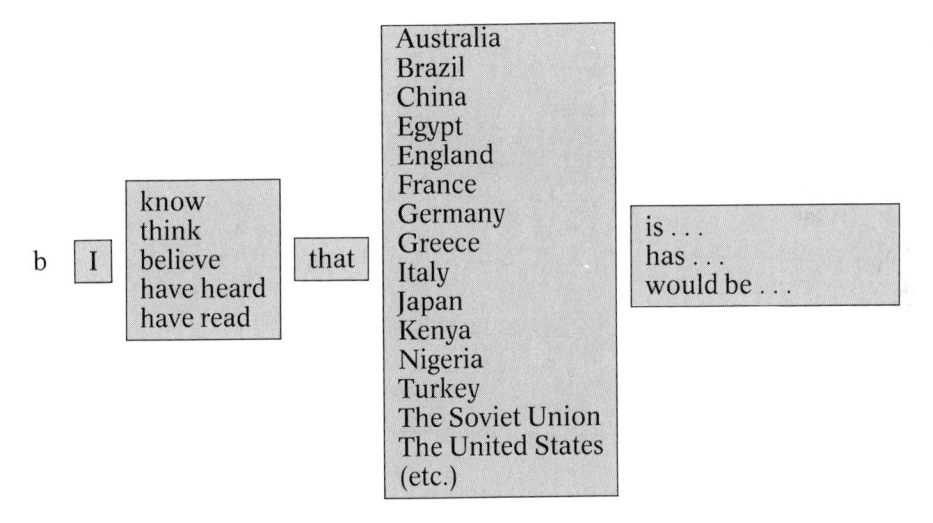

b I | know / think / believe / have heard / have read | that | Australia / Brazil / China / Egypt / England / France / Germany / Greece / Italy / Japan / Kenya / Nigeria / Turkey / The Soviet Union / The United States / (etc.) | is . . . / has . . . / would be . . .

Example: I have heard that Italy has many beautiful old cities, lovely countryside, and friendly people.

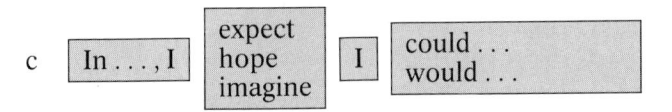

c In . . . , I | expect / hope / imagine | I | could . . . / would . . .

Example: In New York, I imagine I could do lots of exciting things.

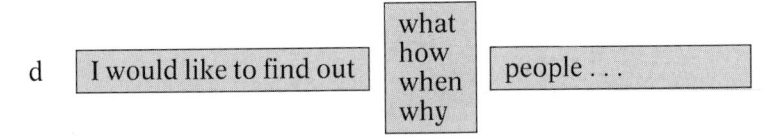

d I would like to find out | what / how / when / why | people . . .

Example: I would like to find out how people live in the villages of India.

51

UNIT TWO: Composition 10

2 Ask and answer
Ask one another the following questions about the country you would like to visit.

a What do you imagine the [people / food / towns / villages / scenery / wild animals / beaches / tourist attractions] [are / is] like?

Example: I imagine French food is very good.

b What kind of things have you heard that [some / many / a few] people in ... [eat? / do? / believe in?]

Example: I have heard that many people in France eat snails.

New structure

In this composition, you are going to practise sentences containing **if clauses (past tense)**.

Example: **If I went** to the United States, **I would visit** New York and San Francisco.

Note: The verb in the **if clause** is in the past tense and the verb in the main clause contains **would**.

3 Complete
If someone offered to pay for a holiday for me, I would feel ...
If I went to ..., I could ...
If I had lots of money ..., ...
If I had some friends in ..., ...

Example: If I went to India, I could visit some friends.

4 Ask and answer

a What would be the advantages if you went to [only one place? / lots of places?]

Example: If I went to only one place, I could see a lot of it and understand a lot about it.

52

b What | would you / could you / might you / ought you to | do if you | had some relatives or friends in ...? / could not speak the language? / lost all your money? / did not like the food in ...? / lost your way in a strange city?

Example: If I had some relatives in America, I would visit them.

c If you could | stop / stay | anywhere you liked, | where would you stay? / where would you stop?

Example: If I could stay anywhere I liked, I would stay in the White House in Washington!

d If you could travel any way you liked, how would you travel?

Example: If I could travel any way I liked, I would travel by ship.

Sample composition

Read through the following:

My imaginary trip around the world

If someone offered to pay all my expenses for a month's holiday anywhere in the world, I would feel very surprised and very excited. It would be difficult to decide where I wanted to go. Should I go to one place or to lots of different places? If I went to one country, I could see and understand a lot about it. If I went to lots of countries, my holiday would be more interesting and more exciting. I think I would decide to fly around the world and to visit three different countries. The countries I would visit would be The United States of America, India and Kenya.

If I went to the United States, I would go there first and stay about a week. I expect I would start by visiting New York. I have heard that New York is a very exciting city. I imagine that there are lots of tourist attractions, that the buildings are spectacular, that the food is very varied and that the people are unfriendly. After I had stayed two or three days in New York, I would fly to San Francisco. I hope I could stay with some relations who live there and I would visit the city and other parts of California.

UNIT TWO: Composition 10

If I went to India, I would stay there for about two weeks. I am sure it would be very interesting to visit a country which is so very different from my own. Before I went, I would write to one of my Indian friends. I would suggest that, if it were possible, he should spend a week with me visiting villages. I would really like to find out how the people live in villages in India. My friend could explain what we saw and he could translate what people said. While I was visiting India, I hope I could also see some of the large cities, such as Delhi and Bombay.

Finally, I would fly to Kenya where I would stay for about a week. There are three things I would like to do in Kenya. First, I hope I could visit the coast because I would like to see the old Arab cities and enjoy the beautiful beaches. Next, I would like to visit a Game Reserve. I imagine the wild animals of Africa – such as the lion, elephant and hippopotamus – are very exciting and beautiful. Finally, I would like to visit the Mountains of Kenya where you can see snow on the Equator.

If someone offered me this money, I would be amazed. Unfortunately, I do not think this will ever happen and I doubt if I shall ever visit these countries.

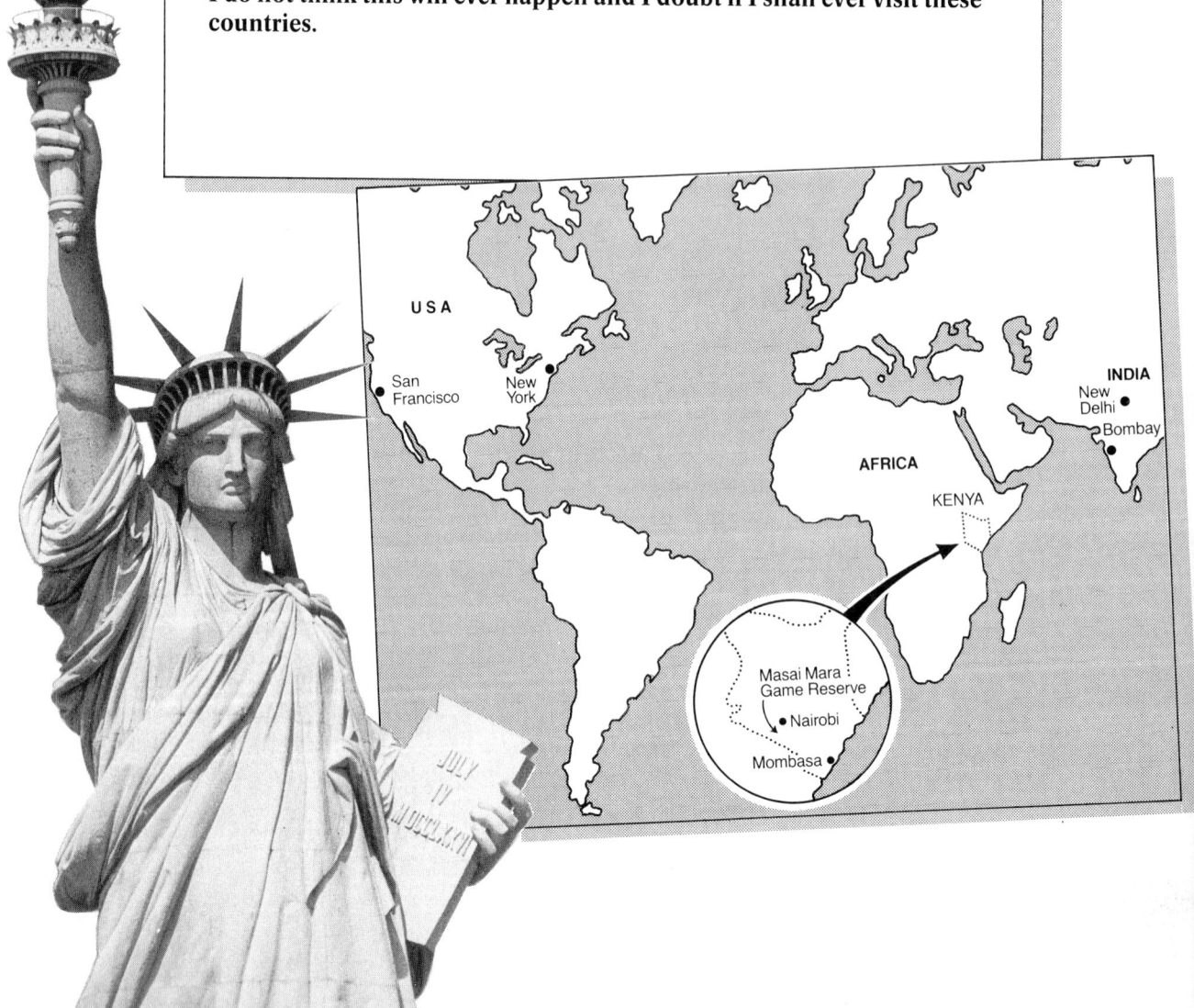

UNIT TWO: Composition 10

Preparation and writing

1 **Structure practice**
   a Choose some sentences from the Structure Practice which you will be able to use in your composition.
   b Write them down in the order in which you will use them.

2 **Sample composition**
   a The Sample Composition has five paragraphs. What is each paragraph about?

Example: *Paragraph one – feelings.*
   – advantages and disadvantages of visiting one or lots of places.
   – final choice.

   b Write down a sentence containing an *if* clause (past tense) from paragraphs 1, 2, 3, 4 and 5.

3 **Your writing**
   a Read the subject on page 50.
   b Think about the holiday you would like to have. Decide how many paragraphs you are going to write.
   c Make notes on the contents of each paragraph. Decide when you will use the sentences you have written from the Structure Practice (1b above).
   d You may find it useful to refer to the Sample Composition while you are writing. Making sure you include several sentences containing an *if* clause (past tense) in your composition.

4 **Checking your work**
   a Read through your writing carefully.
   b Exchange your work with another student.
   c Check each other's work for any mistakes.

UNIT TWO

Composition

11

Subject: **A letter giving travel instructions**

Write a letter to a friend or relation who is coming to stay with you for a holiday. Explain in detail the various ways he/she can travel to your home and suggest which one you think is best. Write about some of the things you hope to do together and describe some of the places you are planning to visit.

Introducing the subject

Have you any friends or relations who live a long way from you?
Where does he/she live?
Is there someone you would like to invite to stay with you?
How long does the journey take?
How would he/she travel?

Structure practice

Imagine you are talking to this friend or relation about his/her visit. Who is coming to visit you? From where are they coming?

Revision

Noun clauses from Compositions Eight and Nine

1 Complete

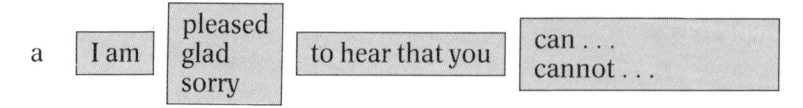

a | I am | pleased / glad / sorry | to hear that you | can... / cannot...

Example: I am glad to hear that you can stay for ten days.

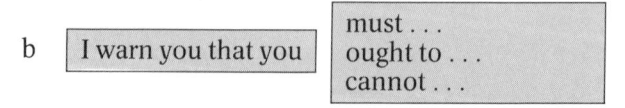

b | I warn you that you | must... / ought to... / cannot...

Example: I warn you that you must book at least a week in advance.

c | It is a pity that you | must... / cannot...

Example: It is a pity that you must leave so early.

d   I wonder if you could . . .

Example: I wonder if you could stay for two weeks.

e | You | ought to / must / can | decide / let me know / warn me / tell me | how . . . / when . . . / where . . . |

Example: You must let me know when you are arriving.

New structure

In this composition, you are going to practise sentences containing **if clauses (present tense)**.

Examples: **If** you **are coming** next week, you **must book** a seat immediately.
If you **let** me know when your train arrives, I **will meet** you at the station.

Note: In these sentences the verb in the **if clause** is in the present tense.

2   Complete

a | If you are coming next week, / If you have to book a seat, / If you want to save some money, | you | must . . . / ought to . . . / may . . . / can . . . |

Example: If you want to save some money, you ought to travel by bus.

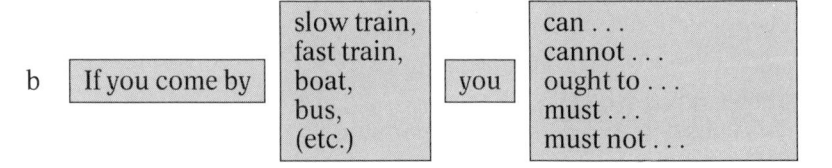

b | If you come by | slow train, / fast train, / boat, / bus, / (etc.) | you | can . . . / cannot . . . / ought to . . . / must . . . / must not . . . |

Example: If you come by slow train, you ought to take some sandwiches and some cold drinks with you.

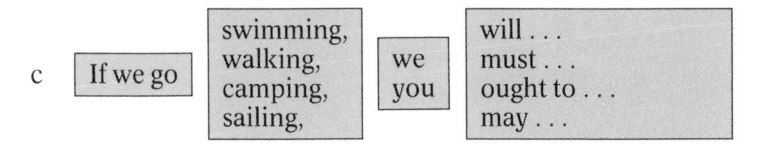

c | If we go | swimming, / walking, / camping, / sailing, | we / you | will . . . / must . . . / ought to . . . / may . . . |

Example: If we go walking, we will need to have heavy boots.

57

UNIT TWO: Composition 11

Revision

Adjectival clauses from Compositions Four and Five

3 Complete

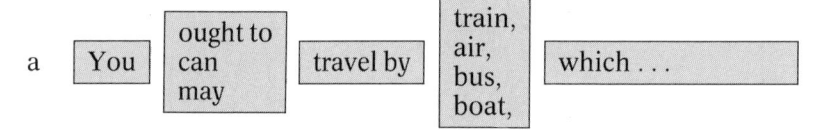

a | You | ought to / can / may | travel by | train, air, bus, boat, | which ...

Example: You can travel by train, which is very fast and comfortable.

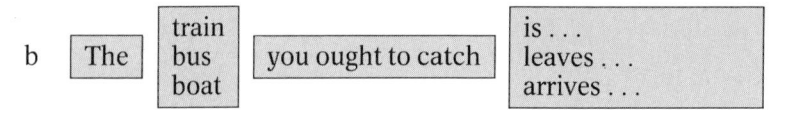

b | The | train / bus / boat | you ought to catch | is ... / leaves ... / arrives ...

Example: The train you ought to catch leaves very early in the morning.

c | On your way, you | must / may / ought to | stop | in ..., / at ..., | which | has ..., / is ...,

Example: On your way, you ought to stop at Tintern, which has a very beautiful old, ruined abbey.

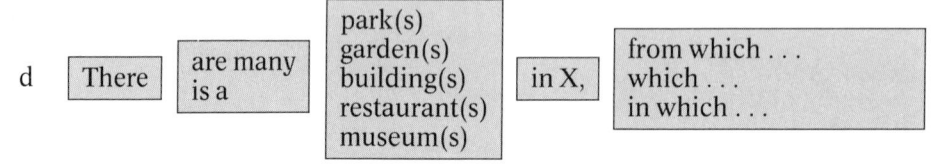

d | There | are many / is a | park(s) / garden(s) / building(s) / restaurant(s) / museum(s) | in X, | from which ... / which ... / in which ...

Example: There is a museum in Monmouth, in which you can see many interesting things.

General revision

Ask and answer
Imagine your friend has asked you the following questions. Answer them in as many ways as possible and make up similar questions of your own.

a | Why | can / may | the journey be very tiring?

Example: The journey can be very tiring because the bus is often late in leaving and in arriving.

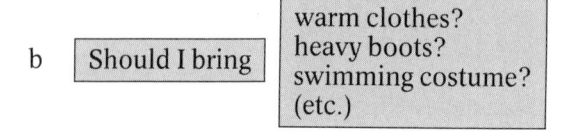

b | Should I bring | warm clothes? / heavy boots? / swimming costume? / (etc.)

58

Answer: You should bring . . .   because . . .
         so that . . .

Example: You should bring heavy boots so that we can go walking on the hills.

c Where should I get off the train?
                               bus?

Example: You should get off the train at Newport.

Sample composition

Read through the following:

Susan and Christine are school friends. Susan has gone to stay at her cottage in Wales for the summer holidays. Susan wrote a letter to Christine inviting her to come and stay with her for two weeks. Christine has written a letter accepting Susan's invitation and asking for advice on the best way to get from London to Wales. This is the letter which Susan wrote in reply to Christine's letter.

> Orchard Cottage,
> Rockfield,
> Monmouth, Wales
> 28th July
>
> Dear Christine,
>
> Thanks very much for your letter which arrived this morning. I am very pleased that your parents have agreed to let you come here and stay for a short holiday. But I am sorry that you can only stay for one week. There is so much to do here that a week is really not long enough. Try to persuade your parents to let you stay for two weeks. If you can stay for only one week, we can do a lot of things. But if you can stay for two weeks, we will be able to do so much more.
>
> In your letter, you ask me for advice on the best way to travel from London. You have a choice of train or coach. If you come by train, you will get here more quickly and also it is very comfortable. The high-speed trains take only an hour and a half from London to Newport, which is quite near here. If you come by coach, it takes a little longer. But, of course, it is much cheaper.

UNIT TWO: Composition 11

If you decide to come by train, then you have to start your journey at Paddington Station. There is a good train from Paddington at 10 o'clock in the morning. It arrives at Newport at 11.30. If you decide to come on this train and if you let me know the day you are coming, we will come in the car to meet you there. It is about an hour's drive from Newport to Rockfield.

If you are coming by coach, you have to catch the coach at Victoria Coach Station. There is an express coach which leaves every weekday at 9.00 a.m. But this coach is always busy in the summer and you have to book a seat in advance. Buy a ticket for Chepstow, which is the first stop, and get off the coach there. It is just under an hour's drive to Chepstow from Rockfield — so it is not very far away from us. Again, if you let me know the day you decide to travel, we will be able to come and meet you. Write me a quick letter or you can give me a ring on 056 754 341.

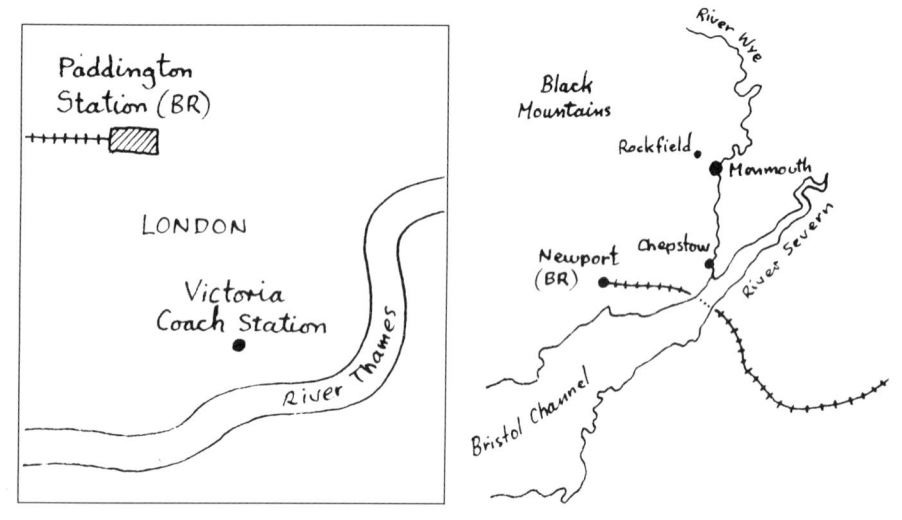

There is so much we can do here. We have just bought a canoe and we can go canoeing on the River Wye. Also, the Black Mountains are very near and we can go walking and climbing. You should bring your swimming things and also boots for walking. I am looking forward very much to your arrival. We shall have lots of fun together. Do try to persuade your parents to let you stay for two weeks. Write soon or give me a ring.

Best wishes,
Susan

Preparation and writing

1 **Structure practice**
   a Choose some sentences from the Structure Practice which you will be able to use in your composition.
   b Write them down in the order in which you will use them.

2 **Sample composition**
   Re-read the Sample Composition.
   a The Sample Composition is a personal letter. Study the diagram.

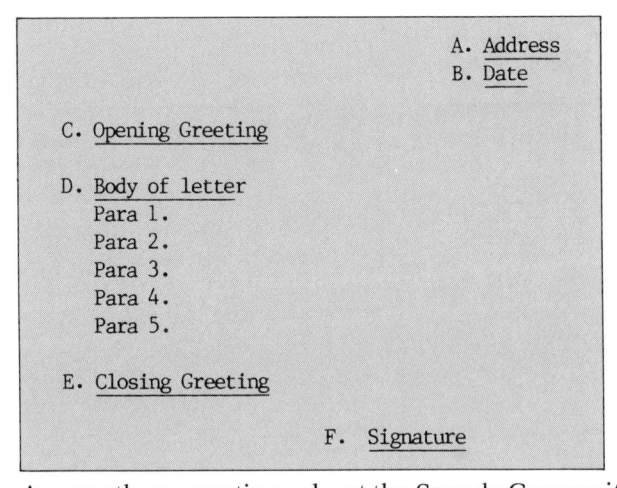

```
                                      A. Address
                                      B. Date

    C. Opening Greeting

    D. Body of letter
       Para 1.
       Para 2.
       Para 3.
       Para 4.
       Para 5.

    E. Closing Greeting

                        F. Signature
```

   Answer these questions about the Sample Composition.
   i What is the writer's address?   ii What is the date?
   iii What is the opening greeting? iv What is each paragraph about?
   v What is the closing greeting?   vi How does the letter end?

   b Write down one sentence containing an *if* clause from paragraphs 1, 2, 3, 4 and 5.

3 **Your writing**
   a Read the subject on page 56.
   b Think about where you live and where your friend has to travel from. What are the different ways he/she can travel? Decide how many paragraphs you are going to write in the letter and make short notes of what you are going to say in each paragraph.
   c Make sure you use several sentences containing *if* clauses in your composition. Include the sentences you have written from the Structure Practice (1b above). You may find it useful to refer to the Sample Composition while you are writing.

4 **Checking your work**
   a Read through your writing carefully.
   b Exchange your work with another student.
   c Check each other's work for any mistakes.

UNIT TWO

Composition 12

Planning and writing a free composition

Planning

Read the Planning section of Composition Six again. Then study the Notes for Composition Seven on this page.

Example: **Notes for Composition Seven:**

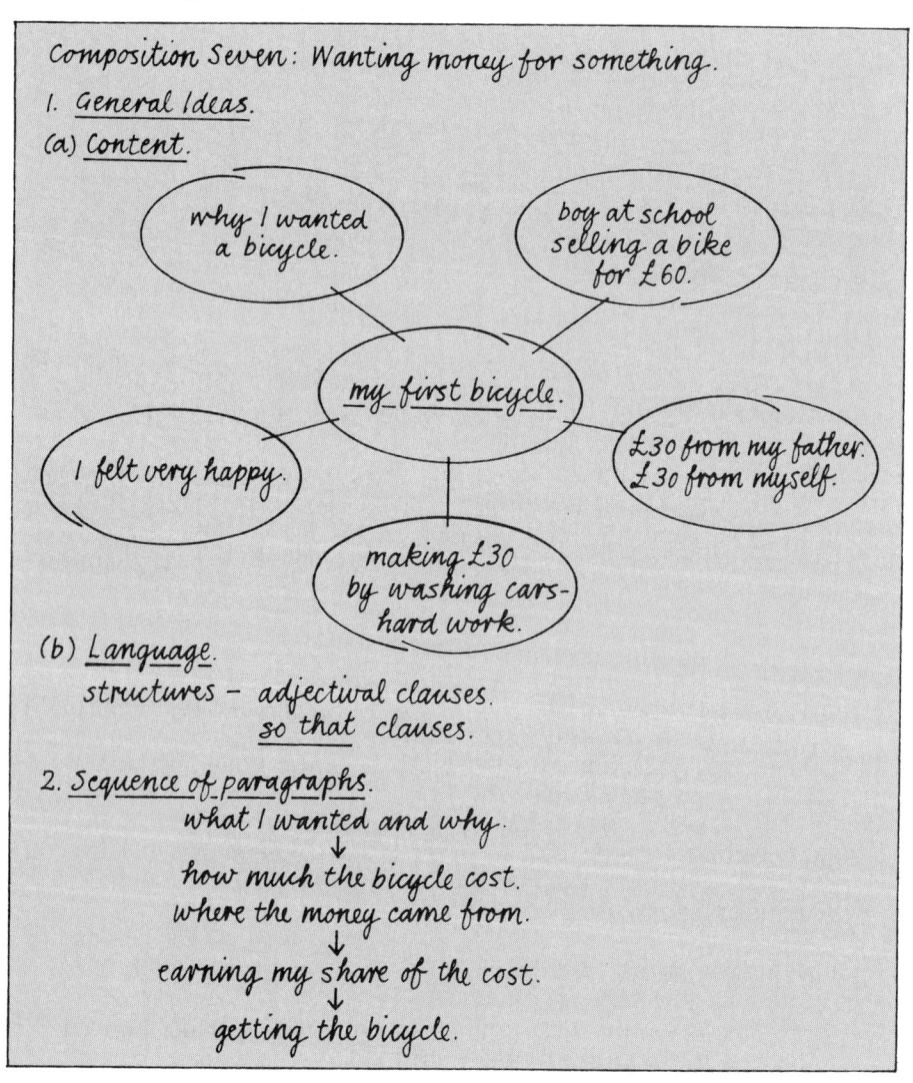

Composition Seven: Wanting money for something.
1. General Ideas.
(a) Content.

- why I wanted a bicycle.
- boy at school selling a bike for £60.
- my first bicycle.
- I felt very happy.
- £30 from my father. £30 from myself.
- making £30 by washing cars – hard work.

(b) Language.
    structures – adjectival clauses.
               so that clauses.

2. Sequence of paragraphs.
    what I wanted and why.
    ↓
    how much the bicycle cost.
    where the money came from.
    ↓
    earning my share of the cost.
    ↓
    getting the bicycle.

Exercise 1: general ideas
Make notes as in the example for (a) content and (b) language for either Composition Eight or Composition Ten. Make notes for either your own composition or for the Sample Composition.

Exercise 2: sequence of paragraphs
Make notes as in the example or look at your notes for Sample Compositions Nine and Eleven. What is the sequence based on – chronological order, topics or a mixture of both?

Kinds of writing

Compositions usually contain the following general kinds of writing:

narrative	– telling an account of what happened, when and why
descriptive	– describing places, people, things, etc.
	– describing events
	– describing processes
discursive	– discussing facts, opinions and feelings

These three kinds of writing often occur in the same composition. For example, Sample Composition Two is mainly a narrative account of a journey across North America, but it contains some descriptive sentences about towns in North America.

Exercise 3
1 Read your compositions for Unit One – Compositions One to Five. Decide what kind of writing they contain:
    Is each composition mostly narrative or mostly descriptive?

2 Read your compositions for Unit Two – Compositions Seven to Eleven. Decide what kind of writing they contain:
    Is each composition mostly narrative, descriptive or discursive?
    Or is each composition a mixture of two or three kinds of writing?

Making your composition interesting

Good descriptive writing can often make your compositions more interesting to read. Can you find any examples of detailed descriptions in your compositions? Remember also that describing things and places in detail gives you lots to write about.

Your writing

Choose *one* of the following subjects for your composition.

1 Describe something exciting, amusing or frightening which happened to you when you were a child and which you remember clearly.

2 Write a letter to a friend about what you are planning to do during your next holiday, and invite your friend to do it with you. If you prefer, you can write about something imaginary which you would like to do and ask your friend if he/she thinks it would be possible.

3 Describe how you succeeded in your education in spite of difficulties.

Before you begin planning your composition, look back at the Structure Practices for Compositions Six to Eleven.

First, write down your general ideas for (a) content and (b) language. Make notes like the ones in the example for Composition Seven.

Second, decide on the sequence for your composition. Make notes of the sequence of paragraphs. Decide first whether the sequence will be in chronological order or in a series of topics.

Third, write two or three sentences that you may use in each paragraph. Try to write some sentences containing time clauses, because clauses, adjectival clauses, *so that* clauses, noun clauses and *if* clauses.

Fourth, write the first draft of your composition. Remember to include some sentences containing detailed descriptions where they are appropriate.

Fifth, read your draft composition, correct it and improve it.

Sixth, make a final copy of your composition.

Your progress

Do you think you are making progress in your composition writing? Compare your earlier compositions with your later compositions.

1 Count the number of words in your Composition Two and the number of words in your Composition Ten. Is your Composition Ten longer? By how much?

2 Count the number of sentences in your Composition Three which contain one or more subordinate clauses. Do the same count for Composition Nine or Eleven. How much of an increase is there?

3 Read the first paragraphs of your Compositions One and Ten. Are you finding it easier to start writing a composition?

UNIT THREE

Composition 13

Subject: **Young people starting work**

At what age are young people allowed to leave school in your country? If they leave school, what sort of jobs can they find? Discuss the subject of employment and unemployment for young people. Then describe what two or three young people you know have done after they left school.

UNIT THREE: Composition 13

Introducing the subject

At what age are young people allowed to leave school?
Can they find jobs easily or is employment a problem?
What sort of jobs can they find?
Do you know anyone who has left school recently?
Do you know anyone who could not find a job?

Structure practice

Revision

Noun clauses from Compositions Eight and Nine

1 Complete

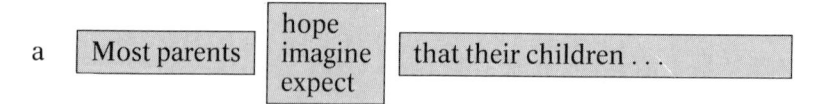

a | Most parents | hope / imagine / expect | that their children ...

Example: Most parents hope that their children will find good jobs.

b It is a pity that many students who want to ...

Example: It is a pity that many students who want to stay at school have to leave and start work.

c | The problem for many young people is that | they ... / there ...

Example: The problem for many young people is that there is a lot of unemployment.

d | Many young people | know / ask their parents / do not know | where ... / what ...

Example: Many young people do not know where they will work when they leave school.

e | My friend, Y, / Someone I know, called Y, | said ... / hoped ... / dreamed ... / thought ...

Example: My friend, Elizabeth, thought she would like to become a doctor.

UNIT THREE: Composition 13

f | A teacher / A careers officer | warned / advised | him / her / us | that ...

Example: A careers officer warned her that she must pass her exams.

Revision

If clauses from Compositions Ten and Eleven

2 **Ask and answer**

a | What can a student do if | he / she | fails the entrance examination to ...? / does badly at school?

Example: If a student does badly at school, she can study again when she is older.

b | What would you advise a friend to do if he/she asked you | what kind of job he/she should get? / where he/she should go to find work? / if he/she should leave school?

Example: If a friend asked me what kind of job she should get, I would advise her to find work she enjoyed doing.

New structure

In this composition, you are going to practise sentences containing clauses joined by **either ... or, and, but** and **so**.

Examples: Young people can **either** remain in full-time education **or** they can try to find a job.
Sandra worked hard **and** did well.
I wanted to leave school, **but** my parents would not allow me.
Simon did badly at school, **so** he wanted to leave.

These clauses are called **co-ordinate clauses**.

3 **Complete**

a | When a young person is ... years old, | he / she | can either ... or ...

Example: When a young person is sixteen years old, he can either leave school or stay on at school to get better qualifications.

b | Most parents would like to keep their children at school | and ... / , but ...

Example: Most parents would like to keep their children at school, but sometimes they do not have enough money.

67

UNIT THREE: Composition 13

c   [Some / Many / A few] [students would like to stay at school] [and . . . / , but . . .]

Example: Many students would like to stay at school and pass the university entrance examination.

d   [Many students] [pass / take / fail] [the secondary school] [entrance / final] [examination] [and . . . / , but . . . / , so . . .]

Example: Many students fail the secondary school final examination and leave school without any qualifications.

e   [If someone has] [bad / good] [exam results,] [he / she] [can either . . . or . . .]

Example: If someone has good exam results, she can either go to university or get a job.

4: Complete
Put in the name of a friend or someone you know for Y and use 'he' or 'she'.

a   [Y thought that school was a waste of time] [, so / and / , but] [he / she] [wanted . . . / imagined . . . / did not know . . .]

Example: My friend thought school was a waste of time, but he did not know what he wanted to do.

b   [Y got a job as] [a / an] [shop assistant / labourer / computer operator / waiter / secretary / telephonist / civil servant / accountant / (etc.)] [and . . . / , but . . . / , so . . .]

Example: Peter got a job as a waiter, but he found that the work was hard and badly paid.

c   [Y got a job] [in a large shop / in a garage / in a building company / in a lawyer's office / with a bank / with the local council / (etc.)] [and . . . / , but . . . / , so . . .]

Example: Sandra got a job in a lawyer's office and she found the work very interesting.

UNIT THREE: Composition 13

d Y could   either . . .   or he/she could . . .
             neither . . .   nor could he/she . . .

Example: Mary could either take the job with a bank or she could go to college.

Sample composition

Read through the following:

Employment for young people in Britain

   Young people in Britain have to stay at school until they are sixteen years old. At sixteen, they can either remain in full-time employment, or they can try to find a job. The problem for young people who want to find a job is that there is a lot of unemployment in Britain.
   The choice that young people can make depends more and more upon their final examination results. If someone has done well at school and has good examination results, he or she has a wide choice. If someone has done badly at school, he or she has very little choice. The young person who has good results can either continue in full-time education or can often find a job with an employer such as a big shop, or bank, or the public services, or in industry. The girl or boy who has poor examination results often wants to leave school, but he or she finds it very difficult to find a job at all. These school leavers often remain unemployed and they have either nothing to do or they go on a government training and work experience scheme. The problem is that there are not enough jobs in Britain for all the school leavers so young people without qualifications have great difficulty. I am going to illustrate these possibilities for young people by telling you about two young people I know.
   Sandra got quite good exam results when she was sixteen, but she had not enjoyed school. She knew that she wanted to leave school. Her careers teacher advised her that she should apply to a large chain of shops or a bank. She got a job with a large chain of shops and started work as a trainee. She worked hard and her manager asked her whether she would like to move to another branch so that she could have wider experience. After she had been at the second shop for a year, she was made a trainee manager and she went to college for one day a week. She continued to do well at work and college so she was made an assistant manager at the age of nineteen.

UNIT THREE: Composition 13

> The story of Simon is not so happy. Simon did badly at school, so he wanted to leave. He thought that school was a waste of time and imagined he would be much happier if he left. He thought he could earn some money and do some of the things he wanted to do. He left school, but he could not find a job, so he went on a government training and work experience scheme. The scheme was in a large garage, but he was not interested in the work, so he did not do well. At the end of the scheme, he still could not get a job. Simon is still unemployed, so he is getting more and more bored. His parents are very worried, but they do not know what they can do.
>
> The present position of many young people who want to leave school at sixteen is very difficult because of unemployment. The result is that more and more young people either stay at school or go into government training schemes, but the problem of unemployment remains.

Preparation and writing

1 **Structure practice**
   a Choose some sentences from the Structure Practice which you will be able to use in your composition.
   b Write them down in the order in which you will use them.

2 **Sample composition**
   a The Sample Composition has five paragraphs. What is each paragraph about?

Example: *Paragraph One — the law about leaving school.*
— introduction to the subject.

   b From the Sample Composition, write down two sentences each containing clauses joined by **and**, **but**, **so**, and **either . . . or**. (eight sentences altogether).

3 **Your writing**
   a Read the subject on page 65.
   b Think about employment and unemployment for young people in your country. Make notes on the main issues. Then decide on the two or three people you are going to write about. Decide how many paragraphs you are going to write.
   c Make notes on the contents of each paragraph. Decide when you will use the sentences you have written from the Structure Practice (1b above).
   d You may find it useful to refer to the Sample Composition while you are writing. Make sure you include several sentences containing co-ordinate clauses in your composition.

4 **Checking your work**
   a Read through your writing carefully.
   b Exchange your work with another student.
   c Check each other's work for any mistakes.

UNIT THREE

Composition 14

Subject: **A strange story**

Most people do not believe in ghosts, but many people have had some sort of strange experience in their lives which they cannot easily explain. Tell the story of something which has happened to you or to someone you know which is not easily explained.

Introducing the subject

Have you ever seen anyone do something and you couldn't understand how they did it?
What happened and why were you puzzled?
Do you know anyone who can do strange things? What sort of things?
Have you ever seen a ghost or do you know anyone who has?
What happened?

Structure practice

Revision

If clauses from Compositions Ten and Eleven

1 **Ask and answer**

What would you do if you | saw a spaceship land?
saw a ghost in a lonely street?
were alone in a ruined house at night?
were with a few friends in a lonely place and heard strange noises?

Revision

Noun clauses from Composition Eight and Nine

2 **Complete**

a | My story is about how | I . . .
Y . . .

Example: My story is about how I heard strange noises in the night.

71

UNIT THREE: Composition 14

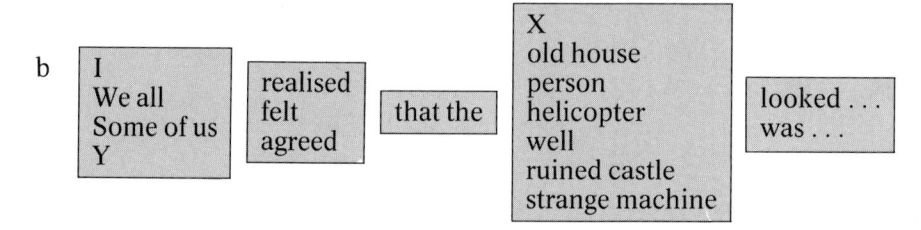

b [I / We all / Some of us / Y] [realised / felt / agreed] [that the] [X / old house / person / helicopter / well / ruined castle / strange machine] [looked ... / was ...]

Example: We all agreed that the person looked very strange.

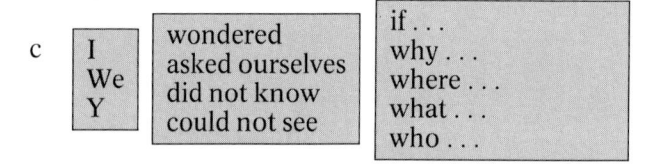

c [I / We / Y] [wondered / asked ourselves / did not know / could not see] [if ... / why ... / where ... / what ... / who ...]

Example: We asked ourselves what the man was doing down by the river.

Revision

Co-ordinate clauses from Composition Thirteen

3 **Complete**

a [I am / Y is] [not easily frightened,] [but ... / so ...]

Example: I am not easily frightened, but this man near our camp worried me a lot.

b [I / Y] [could either ... or ...]

Example: I could either do nothing or go down to the river to see what he was doing.

c [I / Y] [was afraid] [I / he/she] [would be seen,] [but ... / so ...]

Example: Bill was afraid he would be seen, so he crept along quietly on the ground.

d [I / Y] [could neither shout for help nor could] [I ... / he ... / she ...]

Example: I could neither shout for help nor could I run away.

72

UNIT THREE: Composition 14

e | I / Y | shouted loudly for help, but . . .

Example: Peter shouted loudly for help, but no one heard him.

f | This strange experience might have been in | my / his / her | imagination, or it . . .

Example: This strange experience might have been in my imagination, or it might have really happened.

New structure

In this composition, you are going to practise sentences containing **present participle phrases**.

Example: **Feeling tired,** I decided not to pitch my tent, but to sleep in the old house.

4 Complete

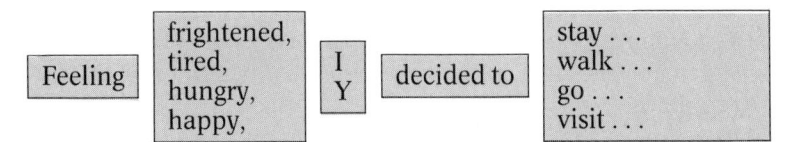

Feeling | frightened, tired, hungry, happy, | I / Y | decided to | stay . . . walk . . . go . . . visit . . .

Example: Feeling hungry, I decided to walk to the village and buy some food.

Ask and answer

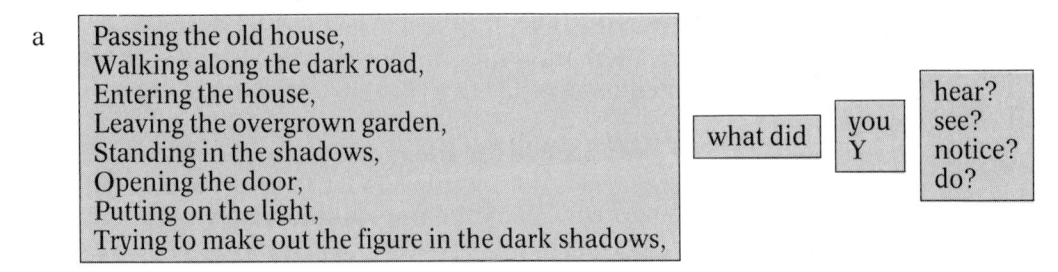

a | Passing the old house,
Walking along the dark road,
Entering the house,
Leaving the overgrown garden,
Standing in the shadows,
Opening the door,
Putting on the light,
Trying to make out the figure in the dark shadows, | what did | you / Y | hear? see? notice? do?

Example: Passing the old house, I heard strange laughter.

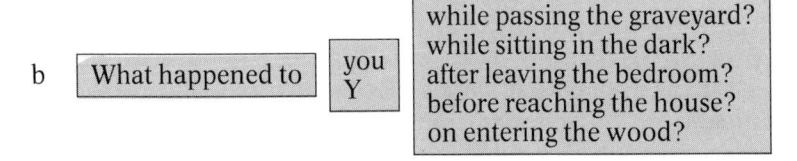

b | What happened to | you / Y | while passing the graveyard?
while sitting in the dark?
after leaving the bedroom?
before reaching the house?
on entering the wood?

Example: While passing the graveyard, I saw a dark figure moving among the graves.

73

UNIT THREE: Composition 14

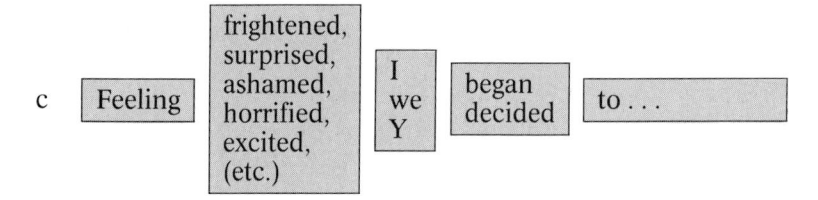

c | Feeling | frightened, surprised, ashamed, horrified, excited, (etc.) | I / we / Y | began / decided | to . . .

Example: Feeling ashamed, we decided to tell no one what we had done.

Sample composition

Read through the following:

My strange story

I used to go camping every summer with some friends. One summer, when I was fourteen years old, something happened which I have never been able to explain.

Four of us set off from our town early one morning. After walking for about fifteen miles, we reached the place where we were going to camp. The campsite was on a high bank of a river. Running through the campsite, a path went down to the river where there was a very deep pool. On the other side of the deep pool, there was a steep cliff. If anyone wanted to visit this part of the river, they had to go there by the path through the campsite. There was only one way back and that was through the campsite. It was neither possible to walk along the bank nor to cross the river.

After pitching our tents, we lit a fire and made a meal. While we were eating our supper, we noticed a man coming towards the campsite. He went past us, but he did not look at us and walked slowly down the path, which led to the river. We all felt that this man looked very strange, but no one said anything because each one of us was afraid of looking stupid.

Finishing our supper, we collected the plates together so that we could take them down to the river to wash them. Walking down the path towards the river, we suddenly stopped and stood looking at each other. We felt afraid because the man who had walked past us had not returned. Feeling ashamed that we were frightened, we began to discuss the man. We all agreed that he had looked very strange and we realised that he must still be beside the deep pool. We stood in silence wondering what he could be doing down by the river.

UNIT THREE: Composition 14

> I suggested we should creep down the path quietly so that we could see what the man was doing. Moving very slowly, we crept down to the river. One boy climbed a tree so that he could see everything clearly. He called out to us that there was no one there. When we got down to the river beside the deep pool, we saw that the boy had been right. There was no one there. Now it was beginning to get dark and we all felt really strange.
>
> Hurrying back up to the campsite, we sat round the fire talking about the man. We wondered who he was and where he had come from. There were no houses near the campsite, only a farm which was about a mile away. But the man had not looked like a farmer. We all thought that perhaps he was a soldier. But we did not know why we thought so. At last, feeling really tired, we all went into our tents and fell asleep. As soon as we woke up, we hurried down to the river, but there was nothing unusual there. We began to wonder if we had imagined the whole thing.
>
> As the days passed, we forgot about the incident. Then one day the farmer who lived nearby came to visit us. We told him the story of the man who had disappeared, wondering if the farmer would laugh at us. However, he did not laugh. He looked astonished and told us that a soldier had committed suicide in that pool just a year ago.
>
> Had we seen a ghost? I do not know.

Preparation and writing

1 **Structure practice**
   a Choose some sentences from the Structure Practice which you will be able to use in your composition.
   b Write them down in the order in which you will use them.

2 **Sample composition**
   a The Sample Composition has eight paragraphs. What is each paragraph about?

Example: *Paragraph One — when the writer had the strange experience.*

   b Write down a sentence containing a present participle phrase from paragraphs 1, 2, 3, 4 and 5.

75

3 Your writing
    a Read the subject on page 71.
    b Think about a strange experience which you or someone you know had. Decide how many paragraphs you are going to write.
    c Make notes on the contents of each paragraph. Decide when you will use the sentences you have written from the Structure Practice (1b above).
    d You may find it useful to refer to the Sample Composition while you are writing. Make sure you include several sentences containing a present participle phrase in your composition.

4 Checking your work
    a Read through your writing carefully.
    b Exchange your work with another student.
    c Check each other's work for any mistakes.

UNIT THREE

Composition

15

Subject: **Sports and games**

Write an account of the different games and the different sports you have played in the past and play now. First, describe in detail one or two games you used to play as a child with your friends. Then describe some of the particular sports you have played or play now. Say whether you like them or not and explain why. Write about one or two sports in detail. You can write about *any* sort of games or sports.

UNIT THREE: Composition 15

Introducing the subject

What is the first game you remember playing as a child? Which games are thought of as 'girls' games' and which as 'boys' games'?
What kind of games did you play during your school holidays?
Which sports did you play while you were at school or college?
Did/do you enjoy sports at school? Why?
Which is your favourite sport or game? Why?

Structure practice

Revision

present participle phrases from Composition Fourteen

1   **Complete**

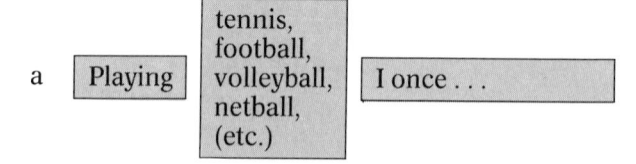

a | Playing | tennis, football, volleyball, netball, (etc.) | | I once . . . |

Example: Playing netball, I once scored twenty points.

b | Running a marathon, Swimming . . . , Cycling . . . , Doing PE . . . , | | I . . . |

Example: Cycling in a 20-kilometre race, I once crashed my bike into a tractor.

c   Describe some games you used to play as a child.

Answer like this: Running around the school playground, we used to play 'catch'.

New structure

In this Composition, you are going to practise sentences containing:

	verb	+	**(pro)noun**	+	**to**	+	**infinitive**	
Example: My friends	persuaded		me		to		play	football with them.

UNIT THREE: Composition 15

2 Complete

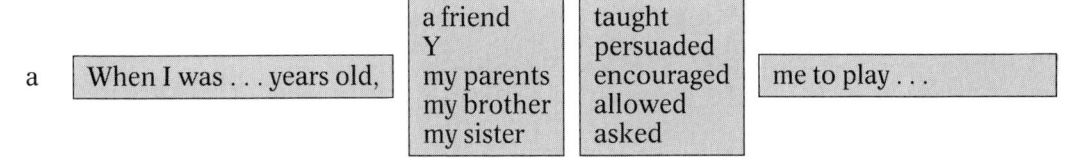

a | When I was ... years old, | a friend / Y / my parents / my brother / my sister | taught / persuaded / encouraged / allowed / asked | me to play ...

Example: When I was nine years old, my sister taught me to play table tennis.

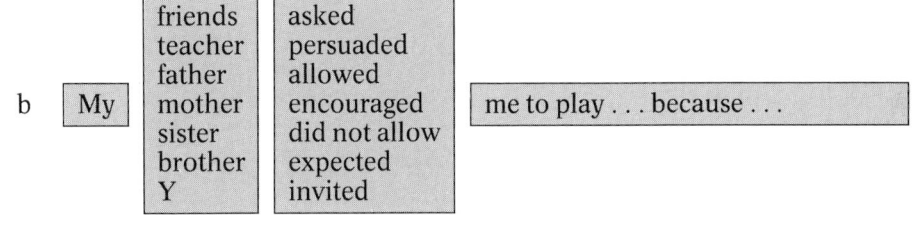

b | My | friends / teacher / father / mother / sister / brother / Y | asked / persuaded / allowed / encouraged / did not allow / expected / invited | me to play ... because ...

Example: My father persuaded me to play golf because he liked it himself.

New structure

In this composition, you are also going to practise sentences containing **although clauses.**

Example: **Although I tried hard to play games at school,** I was never much good at them.

3 Complete
Think of some of the games you used to play when you were a child.

a | Although I liked playing ..., my favourite | game / sport | was ...

Example: Although I liked playing netball, my favourite sport was swimming.

b | Although I did not like climbing trees, / Although my mother warned me to be home early, / Although the river was deep and dangerous, / Although the farmer threatened to punish us, | we ... / Y ... / I ...

Example: Although the farmer threatened to punish us, we used to play hide-and-seek in the corn.

c | Although I was not good at skipping, / Although I didn't like playing hide-and-seek, / Although my friends were always playing ..., / Although my mother wanted me to be home early, | my friends ... / Y ... / I ... / we ...

Example: Although I was not good at skipping, my friends used to persuade me to play with them.

79

UNIT THREE: Composition 15

    d   Think of some of the sports you play now or have played in the past.

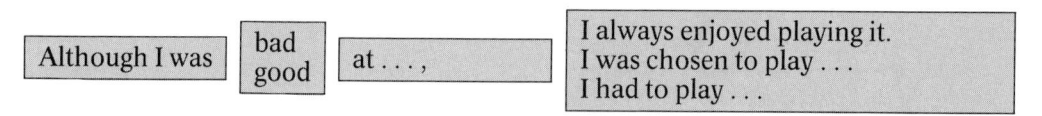

> | Although I was | bad / good | at . . . , | I always enjoyed playing it. / I was chosen to play . . . / I had to play . . . |

Example: Although I was bad at tennis, I was chosen to play for the school team.

    4 Ask and answer
    a   Ask one another the following questions and give as many answers as possible.

What games did you use to play although your parents/teachers had told you not to play them?

Example: Although we were forbidden to play cards, I used to play whist in the classroom.

What sports did you dislike playing although you had to play them at school?

Example: Although I disliked playing football, I had to play it at primary school.

What games did you play as a child which you now think dangerous?

Example: Although it was dangerous, I used to make fires in a wood near our house.

    b | What did you insist on doing / What did your friends persuade you to do / What did you ask your friends to do / What did you like doing | although you knew it was wrong? |

Example: My friends persuaded me to join them in stealing apples although I knew it was wrong.

    5 Complete

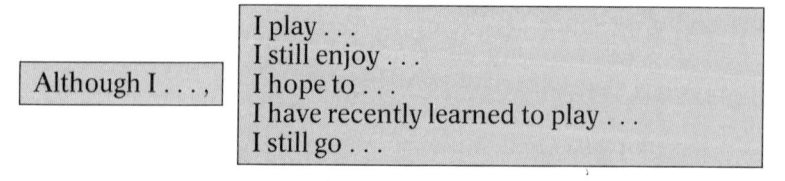

> | Although I . . . , | I play . . . / I still enjoy . . . / I hope to . . . / I have recently learned to play . . . / I still go . . . |

Example: Although I am very busy, I still go swimming twice a week.

Sample composition

Read through the following:

Sports and games

    When I was young, I always enjoyed playing games with my friends. I particularly remember two games I used to play when I was about ten years old. There was a wood surrounding our house. Although the wood seemed big to us children, I suppose it was really quite small. We used to divide into two groups and pretend we were enemies. Then we used to hunt each other in the wood. Hiding behind trees and running silently, we played like this for hours. Afterwards, we used to go to an old hut and light a fire. Unfortunately, one day the hut caught fire. Although we put the fire out quickly, my father ordered us never to make a fire in the hut again. Another game I remember was one we used to play at primary school. Running along the end of the school playing fields, there was a high wall, below which was a pond. We used to see who could run along the wall fastest without falling into the pond. Although we were afraid we might fall into the pond, I expect there was little danger. However, one day a teacher found us playing this game. He ordered us to stop playing and never to do it again.

    I never really enjoyed sports at school because, although I tried hard, I was never much good at the kind of games we had to play. The most common games for boys in English schools are football and cricket. One difficulty was that, although we all had to play these games, we were not really taught properly. Another thing I disliked was that there was always a very strong feeling of competition although teachers always told us to play for enjoyment. But, in fact, students who did well at games were honoured in the school by the teachers. So, naturally, if students were not very good at games, they did not like playing them. Then, one day, playing cricket, I was hit in the face by a cricket ball, which is very hard. Although I was not seriously hurt, this accident made me dislike cricket.

    Now that I am older, I enjoy learning new games and sports. Although I am not particularly good at sports, I can learn if I am taught properly. Recently, a friend persuaded me to learn to play squash. Squash is something like tennis, but it is easier. I could play reasonably well after about four hours' practice.

    Looking back on my schooldays, I feel that the games we used to play on our own were much more enjoyable than the games which were organised by the school. Although it is true that all children should take exercise, I wonder if schools are doing the right thing by forcing students to take part in games they do not like.

UNIT THREE: Composition 15

Preparation and writing

1 **Structure practice**
   a Choose some sentences from the Structure Practice which you will be able to use in your composition.
   b Write them down in the order in which you will use them.

2 **Sample composition**
   a The Sample Composition has four paragraphs. What is each paragraph about?

Example: *Paragraph One — two childhood games.*

   b Write down sentences from paragraphs 1, 2 and 3 containing:
   verb + (pro)noun + *to* + infinitive
   an *although* clause

3 **Your writing**
   a Read the subject on page 77.
   b Think about the different games and sports you used to play. Which ones were organised/ not organised? Which ones did you like/dislike? Decide how many paragraphs you are going to write.
   c Make notes on the contents of each paragraph. Decide when you will use the sentences you have written from the Structure Practice (1b above).
   d You may find it useful to refer to the Sample Composition while you are writing. Make sure you include several sentences containing verb + (pro)noun + *to* + infinitive and several sentences containing *although* clauses in your composition.

4 **Correction**
   a Read through your writing carefully.
   b Exchange your work with another student.
   c Check each other's work for any mistakes.

UNIT THREE
Composition
16

Subject: **An important annual festival**

Write about an important annual festival which you always enjoy. Explain the reasons for this festival and describe in detail the preparations which are made at home and in your town and village for it. Also describe what happens on the actual day.

UNIT THREE: Composition 16

Introducing the subject

What are the main festivals which are celebrated each year in your country?
Which one do you enjoy most?
Do you know the origin of this festival?
When was it first celebrated?
What preparations are made for it?
What do you usually do on the day itself?

Structure practice

Revision

Sentences from Composition Fifteen containing the structure:

	verb	+	(pro)noun	+	to	+	infinitive	
Example: Some friends	**invited**		me		to		visit	them on Christmas Day.

1 Complete

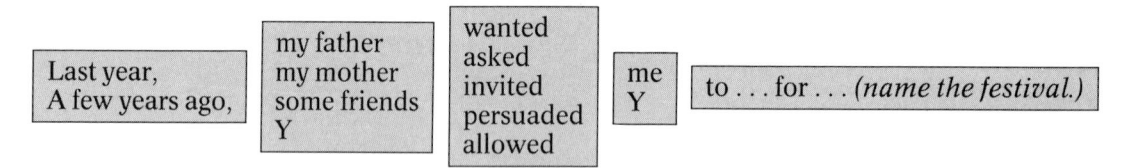

| Last year,
A few years ago, | my father
my mother
some friends
Y | wanted
asked
invited
persuaded
allowed | me
Y | to ... for ... *(name the festival.)* |

Example: Last year, some friends invited me to stay with them for Christmas.

Revision

Although clauses from Composition Fifteen

2 Complete
Although everyone enjoys ..., children ...
Although there is a lot of preparation, ...
Although I usually enjoy ..., I dislike ...
Last year I was given ... although ...
Not everyone can afford to ... although most people would like to.

Example: Although I usually enjoy giving parties, I dislike having to prepare for them.

New structure

In this composition, you are not going to practise a new type of sentence. Instead you are going to practise **passive verbs** in many different types of clauses which you have already used.

Examples: The festival **is called** Christmas because it celebrates the birth of Christ.
Children find their stockings **have been filled** with presents.

UNIT THREE: Composition 16

3 Complete
The festival is called . . . because . . .
The festival is celebrated on . . .
. . . are given by . . . to . . .
New clothes are worn on the occasion of . . .
The special dishes which are prepared are . . .

Example: Presents are given by parents to their children.

4 Ask and answer
Ask one another the following questions about the decorations and preparations which are made for the festival.

a | How | are the streets / is your house | decorated? |

Example: The streets are decorated by putting coloured lights in the trees.

Think of a special dish which is made for the festival.

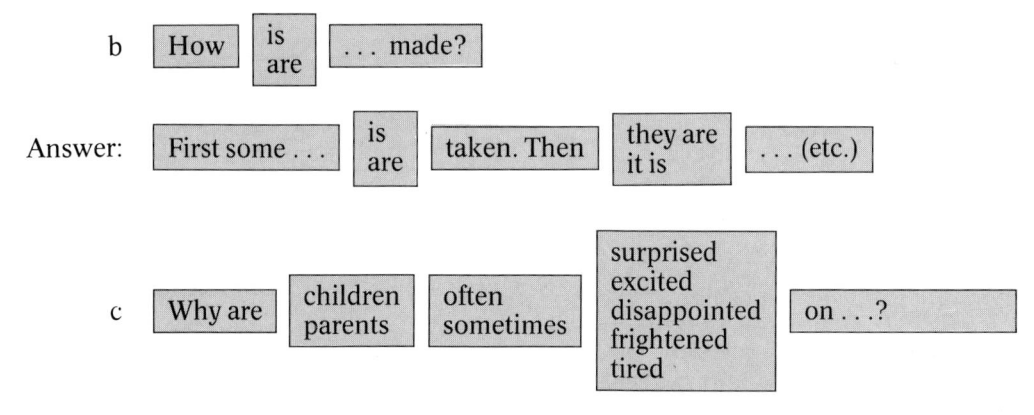

b | How | is / are | . . . made? |

Answer: | First some . . . | is / are | taken. Then | they are / it is | . . . (etc.) |

c | Why are | children / parents | often / sometimes | surprised / excited / disappointed / frightened / tired | on . . . ? |

Example: Children are often tired on Christmas Day because they wake up very early.

d | When are the preparations for . . . | started? / completed? |

Example: The preparations for Christmas are started many weeks before the event.

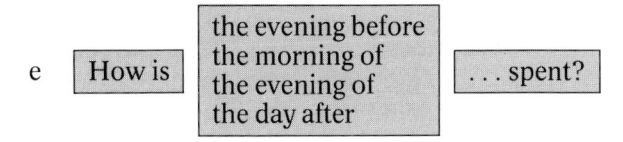

e | How is | the evening before / the morning of / the evening of / the day after | . . . spent? |

Example: The day after Christmas is spent resting and recovering from the celebrations of the previous day.

85

5 Complete

Think of any criticisms which are made about how the festival is celebrated.

a   Although . . . is supposed to be a religious festival, many people complain that . . .

Example: Although Christmas is supposed to be a religious festival, many people complain that it has much more to do with selling and buying than with religion.

b   Although . . . is celebrated on . . . , the preparations are begun . . .

Example: Although Christmas is celebrated on the 25th December, the preparations are begun many weeks before then.

Sample composition

Read through the following:

Christmas in England

Christmas Day, the 25th of December, is the biggest annual festival which is celebrated in England. Although this festival is religious in origin, celebrating the birthday of Jesus Christ, many of the customs and celebrations are not religious. But many people still begin the celebration of Christmas by going to church.

Preparations for Christmas are begun months before the day although many people think it is far too early. Shops are at their busiest in the weeks before Christmas because lots of presents are given, which means that more goods are sold than at any other time of the year. The shops and streets are decorated with bright, coloured lights. Christmas trees, which are large fir trees decorated with lights, are put up in main streets and in squares. A very large Christmas tree, which is given each year by the Norwegian government, is put up in Trafalgar Square, in the centre of London. Because preparations are started so early, some people say they are bored with Christmas before it arrives.

Preparations are also made at home. Special puddings and cakes are eaten on Christmas Day and these are supposed to be cooked three or four weeks in advance. Although it is traditional to cook these in advance, many people do not bother and leave their cooking until the last minute. During the week before Christmas, houses are decorated with coloured paper and with leaves and branches. A small Christmas tree is usually placed in the living room.

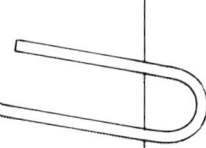

UNIT THREE: Composition 16

> Although most people enjoy Christmas Day, it is particularly enjoyed by children. They get very excited because of the presents they know they will receive. Small children believe that their presents are brought to their rooms during the night by Father Christmas, who is supposed to travel through the sky on a sledge pulled by reindeer. The sledge is loaded with beautiful presents. Stopping on the roofs of houses, Father Christmas is supposed to enter the houses by the chimney and leave the presents for children in their stockings which are hung up by their bedsides. Children are very excited on Christmas morning and wake up early. When they wake up, children find that their stockings have been filled with presents.
>
> Although they may have to travel a long way, people like to spend Christmas with their families. During the days before Christmas, the trains and buses are crowded with people who are travelling home so that they can be with their families on Christmas Day. On Christmas morning, services are held in all churches, which are attended by lots of people. Christmas dinner will be served either in the middle of the day or in the evening. It is a very special meal and usually includes a turkey and Christmas pudding. After finishing dinner, the family give each other presents which have been put on the Christmas tree a few days earlier. After giving and receiving these presents, the family will play games or sit down and talk or watch television.
>
> The day after Christmas Day is called Boxing Day and it is also a holiday. On Boxing Day, people rest quietly after the celebrations of the previous day.

Preparation and writing

1 **Structure practice**
   a Choose some sentences from the Structure Practice which you will be able to use in your composition.
   b Write them down in the order in which you will use them.

2 **Sample composition**
   a The Sample Composition has six paragraphs. What is each paragraph about?

Example: *Paragraph One — the name of the festival, its origin and when it is held.*

   b Write down seven sentences containing a verb in the passive from the Sample Composition.

3 Your writing
a Read the subject on page 83.
b Think about a big annual festival in your country. Decide how many paragraphs you are going to write.
c Make notes on the contents of each paragraph. Decide when you will use the sentences you have written from the Structure Practice (1b above).
d You may find it useful to refer to the Sample Composition while you are writing. Make sure you include several sentences containing a verb in the passive in your composition.

4 Checking your work
a Read through your writing carefully.
b Exchange your work with another student.
c Check each other's work for any mistakes.

UNIT THREE

Composition **17**

Subject: **Changes in your town or village**

In most places, many things have changed in the last fifty years. Things such as electricity, running water, good roads, aeroplanes, new means of communication and more schools have made life easier and pleasanter. Describe some of the ways in which life in your town or village has changed since one of your grandparents, older relations or friends was young. Say whether or not the changes have made life better for those living in your town or village.

Introducing the subject

Do your know any elderly people who talk about life when they were young?
Do they say life was different then?
Do they think life is easier for people today?
Why do they think this?
Do they think some things were better when they were young than they are now?
Do you think life has changed much in the past fifty years? In what ways?
Do you think life is better now or worse?

Structure practice

Revision

Adjectival clauses from Compositions Four and Five

1 Complete

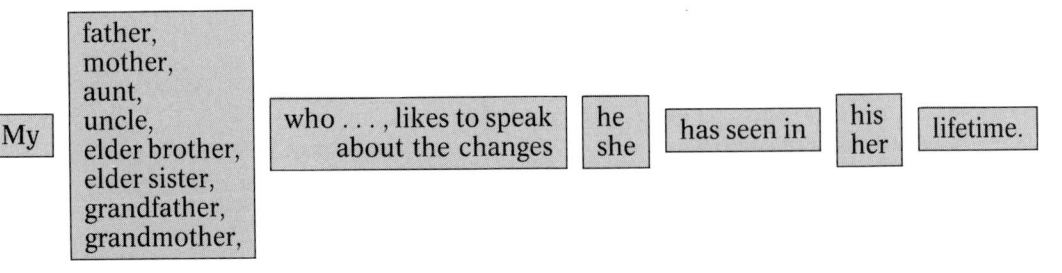

a | My | father, mother, aunt, uncle, elder brother, elder sister, grandfather, grandmother, | who . . . , likes to speak about the changes | he she | has seen in | his her | lifetime.

Example: My grandmother, who is eighty-three years old, likes to speak about the changes she has seen in her lifetime.

89

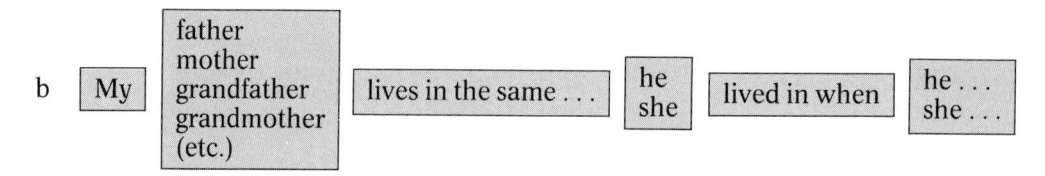

UNIT THREE: Composition 17

b [My] [father / mother / grandfather / grandmother / (etc.)] [lives in the same ...] [he / she] [lived in when] [he ... / she ...]

Example: My grandmother lives in the same house she lived in when she got married.

2 Make a list of changes.

Some of the biggest changes which have taken place in my town/village during the last . . . years are . . .

For each change given in your list, complete the sentence:

Now people can . . . which is . . .

Example: electrification of the railway
Now people can travel by electric train which is much quicker and cleaner.

3 Ask and Answer

[What has happened in your] [town / village] [which has made life] [more / less] [pleasant for older people?]

Example: Two things which have made life less pleasant for older people are the fast traffic and the high cost of heating in winter.

New structure

In this composition, you are going to practise sentences containing **infinitives of purpose**.

Examples: Many things have been done **to make** life easier.
My aunt had to use coal **to heat** water.

4 Complete

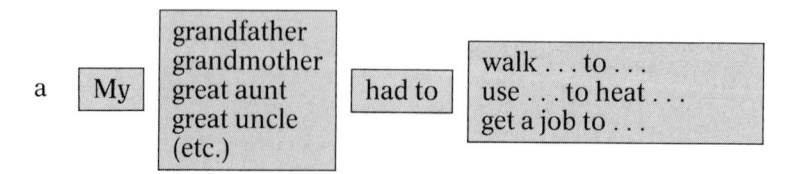

a [My] [grandfather / grandmother / great aunt / great uncle / (etc.)] [had to] [walk ... to ... / use ... to heat ... / get a job to ...]

Example: My grandmother had to walk a hundred metres to get water.

90

b My | grandfather grandmother (etc.) | would have liked | more money / longer holidays / more education / greater freedom (etc.) | to ... when | he / she | was young.

Example: My grandmother would have liked more time at school to get some qualifications when she was young.

5 Ask and answer

a What has been done | to make life pleasanter for everyone? / to provide more education? / to make travel faster and more comfortable? / to provide jobs? / to make houses more comfortable? / to give young people something to do in the evening? / to make life easier for older people?

Example: Free bus travel has been provided to make life easier for older people.

b Why | was a / were | new school(s) built / lot of shops built / new housing estate built / new industrial estate built | in ...?

Example: New schools were built in my grandmother's town to provide better education for the children.

Sample composition

Read through the following:

Changes my grandmother has seen in her lifetime

My grandmother, who is eighty-three years old, lives in the same house she lived in when she was first married. That was more than sixty years ago. She likes to talk about the changes she has seen in her lifetime. There are some things she does not like about modern life; but she agrees that most of the changes she has seen have been for the better. Many things have been done to make life easier for ordinary people.

When she was young, there was no running water or electricity in the house. If she wanted to cook or wash, she had to walk about a hundred metres to get water. If she wanted a bath, she had to bring coal and light a fire. Then she used all the pots and kettles in the house to heat as much water as possible to fill a big tub which was put in the middle of the kitchen. Now that she has running water and electricity, she finds it much easier to do the housework.

Also, she agrees that it is much easier to travel from one place to another. When she was young, it took over an hour to travel to the nearby city in a smoky, noisy train. Now, she can do that same journey in twenty minutes in an electric train, which is much quieter and cleaner. Even walking on the streets of the town was not easy – especially in winter. The house she lived in was on a steep hill and she had to get up and down this hill to do the shopping. Sometimes, when it snowed in winter, she could not get down the hill to the shops for a week or more. Now, many improvements have been made to the roads. Steps have been made with a handrail to make it easier for people to get up and down the hill.

UNIT THREE: Composition 17

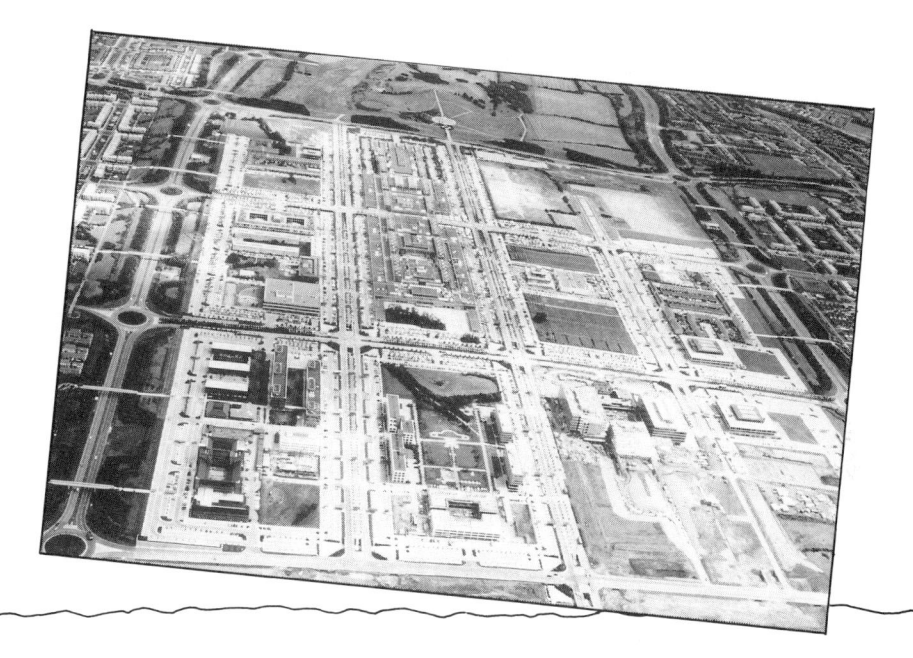

My grandmother often talks about the many new kinds of entertainment which are available. When my grandmother was young, cinemas were just starting and television had not been invented. People had to find ways to entertain themselves in the evenings. She remembers dark winter evenings when she was a child. In the house she lived in then, there was only a gas lamp and an open coal fire. But the children found things to do to keep themselves amused. They played games together and, so my grandmother thinks, were just as happy as children are today.

Nowadays, my grandmother agrees, there are much better opportunities for education. My grandmother had to leave school when she was ten years old to get a job to make extra money to help her parents. My grandmother would have liked more time at school to get some qualifications. These qualifications would have enabled her to get a better job. But she was not able to do this. Today, many new schools have been built to provide a better education for children. Children can stay on at school to get better qualifications.

However, my grandmother points out that some things have changed for the worse. When she was young, the town was small and everybody knew and trusted each other. They did not need to keep their doors locked to keep their houses safe. Everyone was friendly with each other and they helped one another when in need. Nowadays, people have to keep their houses locked to keep their possessions safe. There is no longer the same feeling of people living happily together in a friendly community.

UNIT THREE: Composition 17

Preparation and writing

1 Structure practice
   a Choose some sentences from the Structure Practice which you will be able to use in your composition.
   b Write them down in the order in which you will use them.

2 Sample composition
   a The Sample Composition has six paragraphs. What is each paragraph about?

Example: *Paragraph One — changes in the life of someone who is eighty-three.*
— some changes she does not like.
— many changes for the better.

   b Write down a sentence containing an infinitive of purpose from paragraphs 1, 2, 3, 4, 5 and 6.

3 Your writing
   a Read the subject on page 89.
   b Think about the changes in your town or village in an older person's life since he/she was young. Decide how many paragraphs you are going to write.
   c Make notes on the contents of each paragraph. Decide when you will use the sentences you have written from the Structure Practice (1b above).
   d You may find it useful to refer to the Sample Composition while you are writing. Make sure you include several sentences containing an infinitive of purpose in your composition.

4 Checking your work
   a Read through your writing carefully.
   b Exchange your work with another student.
   c Check each other's work for any mistakes.

UNIT THREE

Composition 18

Free compositions

Planning

Read through the sections in Composition Six and Composition Twelve about planning and kinds of writing.

Subjects

This is a list of subjects for free composition writing.

1 Describe how you decided (or were asked) to organise a visit, a scientific experiment, a meeting, a party or anything else you wish to write about. Say how you persuaded your friends to join in and help you, and describe what happened.

2 Most people disagree with their parents or relatives sometimes. Write about one or more disagreements you have had. Explain why you disagreed and decribe what happened and how it ended. Discuss who you now think was right or wrong.

3 Write about your plans and ambitions for the future. Explain your reasons for these and describe the sort of difficulties you will have to overcome.

4 Describe any crime you have been connected with, have heard about or have read about. Then describe a type of crime which is common in your country and try to explain what, you think, are the reasons.

5 A foreign friend has written a letter to you in which he/she described the celebration of an event in which he/she took part. He/she has asked you to describe the celebration of any important event, either national or local, which you have seen or taken part in. Write a reply to his/her letter. For example, you might write about the celebration of an event of historical importance.

6 Imagine you have been asked to write an article for a foreign newspaper about the opinions and problems of young people in your country. You could discuss subjects like education, music, jobs, marriage and so on. You might also mention how opinions of young people are different from those of older people.

7 In most parts of the world today people are getting much more education than their parents did. Are you one of those people? If so, describe what your parents feel about this situation, and describe any difficulties you have had at home.

8 Retell the story of an interesting experience or historical event which one of your grandparents or another older person told you. Or, describe what you remember about an important event in the history of your country which has taken place in your own life time.

Preparation and writing

Before you begin planning your composition, look back at the Structure Practices for Compositions Thirteen to Seventeen.

First, write down your general ideas for (a) content and (b) language.

Second, decide on the sequence for your composition. Make notes of the sequence of paragraphs. Decide first whether the sequence will be in chronological order or in a series of topics.

Third, write five or six sentences that you may use in each paragraph. Try to write some sentences containing noun clauses, *if* clauses, *although* clauses, co-ordinate clauses, present participle phrases, clauses with verb + (pro)noun + *to* + infinitive and clauses with verbs in the passive.

Fourth, write the first draft of your composition. Remember to include some sentences containing detailed description where they are appropriate.

Fifth, read you draft composition, correct it and improve it.

Sixth, make a final copy of your composition.